MW01230069

Home Buying Made *Easy* for First Time Buyers in Rhode Island

LEGAL NOTICE

Nate Colwell's 5 Step Checklist to a Hassle Free Home Buying Process

Step 1: Before you start your home search, meet with your loan officer to get preapproved. While doing so, you'll want to create a realistic budget and discuss the various loan programs you may qualify for. Doing this up-front will allow you to know how much home you can afford, the types of loans you may qualify for as well as the approximate monthly payment and closing cost you should expect. By securing a pre-approval letter, you will make your house hunting much more enjoyable.

Step 2: Make a list of the amenities you are looking for in a home. You will want to consider location, property type and your must have features. For example, do you want to be close to the city or live in the suburbs? do you want a home with a yard, or would you prefer a condo? Do you need 4 bedrooms, or will 3 bedrooms work well?

Step 3: Select a Real Estate Agent to represent you. An agent is incredibly valuable because they will listen to your needs then research all the available homes that meets your criteria. Often, they will put you on a drip campaign, based on the criteria you provide, of "new-to-market" properties to keep you up to date with available homes.

Step 4: Tour homes that your agent locates and ask questions about each property to ensure it meets your needs and that there is nothing concerning to your agent. Agents tour homes on a regular basis so they may notice things that you miss. Also, make sure to contact your loan officer before making any offer. Your loan officer will be able draft an updated preapproval letter and provide important financial information such as the monthly mortgage payment and closing costs. This will help to ensure the property stays within your budget.

Step 5: Your agent will help you negotiate the offer and inspections. At the same time your loan officer will submit your file and begin the process of getting your mortgage fully approved. After the appraisal, inspections and underwriting, you will be ready to close on your new home!

When you prepare in advance by hiring seasoned professionals, you will have a much more enjoyable home buying experience.

Table of Contents

Preface

Before I write anything else, I want to say thank you for choosing my book to learn about becoming a first-time home buyer. Although a book about real estate and mortgage financing isn't the most exciting topic, it is a very important one. Buying a home is likely the largest financial decision of your life so going into such a large transaction with the information I've included here will be incredibly beneficial to your success in real estate.

If you only take away one thing from this book, I hope it is that *preparation is crucial to the home buying experience*. Furthermore, the best way to prepare is to hire seasoned professionals who have your best interests in mind. No one was born a real estate guru; this type of knowledge is acquired through independent research, experience and working with those that have gone through the process and know what they are doing.

You may notice that there isn't any hyper local real estate information contained within this book and that is because as soon as I put this into print, things could change. The goal of this book is to give you a primer so you can become more educated about the home buying process which has stayed consistent for quite some time.

If you would like more information about certain towns/cities in Rhode Island, please give me a call and I will do my best to answer your questions and/or provide a local real estate agent that can.

I hope you find value in my book and can use this information to purchase the home of your dreams. If I can help you in any way, please don't hesitate to contact me.

Nate Colwell
401-413-3329
Nate.Colwell@Movement.Com

1
Overview

If you are currently living in an apartment or renting a house, you may be thinking about buying a home of your own. This can be an exciting time. But before you start actively looking for a home to purchase, there is some planning that needs to be done. If you do not plan properly for the time, energy and financial exertion that comes along with buying a home, you will be setting yourself up for failure.

Some of the planning will include:
- Choosing a loan officer
- Choosing a real estate agent
- Determining your must-have amenities
- Determining your home size requirements
- Determining your yard size requirement
- Understanding the economics of the housing market
- Research and understand the different types of home utilities (well water vs. public, sewer hookup vs. septic etc.)
- Discussing the financial implications of buying a home with your financial advisor

This list does not include all the decorating, home improvement, and other decisions you will need to make once you have purchased the home. In other words, home ownership can be VERY time consuming. Asking if you have the time to be a homebuyer may be a crucial first question to ask yourself.

If you decide to continue your pursuit of becoming a first-time home buyer, you will be nervous about finding the right home, saving money for a down payment, and getting approved for financing. This is where hiring competent professionals, who have your interest in mind, will be crucial to your home buying experience.

Other considerations that will need to be addressed once you find a home and go under contract include:
- Moving arrangements

- Deciding which pieces of personal property to keep and which will get discarded (you won't realize how much stuff you have until you need to put every item in a moving box)
- Budgeting for any repairs/renovations
- Taking time off from work for your move

Proper planning will help you transition into your new home much easier than if you wait until the last minute to deal with these details. If you are planning on moving yourself, you should find a few friends or family members that will be willing and able to assist you on move-in day.

* **Pro Tip*** Beer and pizza can go a long way when trying to get extra sets of hands on move-in day.

New Homes vs. Older Homes

Another decision you need to make is whether to buy a new home or an older home. Most first time home buyers usually opt for an older home, but this should not deter you from visiting a few builders to see if there are options that fit your budget. The allure of buying brand new is strong but this generally comes with a larger price tag which is a consideration you, your loan officer and financial advisor will need to discuss.

Older homes may cost less, but they will likely require more upkeep and, potentially, some renovations. In this book, you will learn what to look for when visiting open houses, things that may come up on a home inspection and what you and your real estate agent should include in your purchase offer to ensure you protect yourself in case there are any imperfection with the home (There almost always will be some aspect that doesn't fit your criteria).

Which Home to Choose?

After you have investigated all your options, you will be wondering which home to choose. When looking at homes, you should keep these criteria in mind:
- Size
- Price
- Neighborhood
- Mortgage payments
- Required repairs
- Additional features that meet your amenities list

While this is not an exhaustive list, throughout this book we will discuss other considerations associated with finding your dream home.

You may find yourself overwhelmed by all the information available to you and it may come down to that 'gut-feeling' as to whether you put an offer on a home or not. If you've done your homework and prepared yourself properly, you'll likely know when that decision is the right move.

Moving into your first home will be an experience you will never forget. You should be excited about this little piece of the world that is all yours. Whether this is your forever home or a steppingstone to something bigger and better, buying a home will give you a sense of pride and of purpose.

One of the more rewarding moments will be when the seller slides the keys across the closing table and you officially become a homeowner. It's a difficult feeling to describe but one I hope you get to experience. I assure you, all of planning will be worth it when this time arrives.

2
Location, Location, Location

Choosing where to live is almost as important as the type of home you want to live in. While this is a very personal decision, there are pros and cons to every neighborhood. Wherever you want to live, you will need to identify where the highways, grocery stores, schools and your work are in relation to the home. Buying a home means more than the structure you will be living in. It is your central hub of your life and the place in which you will leave in the morning and return in the evening. It's the place that you, your family and your friends will gather for holidays. During your property search, you'll be looking at houses but when it becomes yours, it becomes a home.

Finding the Right Neighborhood

How will you know when you found the right neighborhood? There are many ways to tell:
- You may feel a sense of calm
- The neighborhood may remind you of a happy memory
- You will be close to places you often visit
- The neighborhood aesthetics are pleasing
- Your family feels it will be a great place to celebrate holidays and events

Buying a home is a very emotional experience and one that can bring great joy to you and your family. But as great as buying a home can be for your family, there are potential pitfalls that need to be researched and carefully considered as well.

When looking for the right location, you should consider the following:
- How clean is this neighborhood?
- Is this a high crime area?
- What is the average home value in the neighborhood?
- Are there community bylaws?
- Proximity to amenities?
- Is there garbage/recycling pickup?

While these questions do not cover everything, these are the types of questions you should be thinking about when looking at any home. Seasoned realtors know what questions to ask and will likely ask question you never thought to ask which is why they are an invaluable resource in real estate transactions.

How Clean is this Neighborhood?

You should look at the neighborhood at different times of day to see how those who live in the neighborhood take care of it. If there is a lot of trash on the ground, the yards are not kept up properly, or there are old signs posted on trees and telephone poles, then the neighborhood may not be for you.

If the neighborhood looks clean and you see people outside caring for their lawns, then you may have found a community of people who care about where they live. This is an important factor if you are planning on living in the neighborhood for many years. All too often people will buy homes only to discover that they live in a neighborhood where people do not have respect for their own property or the property of others. This can make selling the home much more difficult in the future.

Is this a High Crime Area?

While all neighborhoods will experience some crime, you should consider buying a home in an area with a low crime rate. While a home in a higher crime rate area may be the right price for your budget, it may not be in an area that is right for your well-being.

Drive by the neighborhood at nighttime to see if there is adequate street lighting, suspicious activity, or anything else that might cause you to use caution. Research the neighborhood and find out how the crime rate compares to other neighborhoods. If the crime rate is too high, then it may be best to look somewhere else.

You can also look up rankings online to find which towns/neighborhoods have the best/worst track records for criminal activity. This information is usually easily accessible through a simple Google search.

What is the Average Home Value in the Neighborhood?

You can find this information very easily by asking your realtor or by researching this information at the town/city clerk's office or on the municipality's web site. You should be aware of the home values that are in your neighborhood for several reasons:

- Housing prices will vary depending on the neighborhood and region. You want to buy a home that will be an appreciating asset.
- You do not want to pay too much for a home.
- Giving a solid offer for the home means knowing what other homes of similar size are selling for. Ask your realtor to complete a Comparative Market Analysis (CMA) to determine what he home may be worth prior to making any offer.

Are there Community Bylaws or HOAs?

If you are looking at a home that is part of a community or homeowners association (HOA), you should be aware of the rules and regulations that everyone who owns property in the HOA must abide by. Many HOAs restrict what can be left in front of the home, such as, RVs or Boats. Some don't allow for clothes lines and others have strict noise guidelines.

Many people enjoy living in an HOA because it creates a true sense of community. HOAs usually have get-togethers and other events during the year where neighbors can socialize. Some communities have pools, tennis courts, and other amenities. Traditionally, you will find these to be townhouses or condominiums but there are single-family neighborhoods/communities that are part of HOAs as well. Many of the new developments have some sort of HOA to cover maintenance expenses (street plowing, streetlight repair/upkeep etc.), landscaping for entrances or other communal areas etc.

Some HOAs also have restrictions on pet types and sizes which can be major consideration for pet lovers.

When considering any home, ask if there is an HOA at your initial showing. If there is, ask for a copy of the rules & regulations along with the by-laws. Most listing agents should have this information readily available at the open house or showing appointment.

Proximity to Amenities?

When choosing a home, you will need to find the nearest grocery stores, schools, route to work, and other necessities that will make living in the neighborhood more convenient. Drive around the neighborhood to see what is close by and what must-have amenities are further away. It's likely you will never find a home that is in perfect proximity to EVERYTHING you would like so you'll need to prioritize what is most important for you.

Is there Garbage/Recycling Pickup?

Trash pick-up may seem like a trivial concern but for those that do not have regular waste pickup (generally in more rural areas), they need to make trips to the landfill or get a dumpster rental at their home. These are the details that can be overlooked when buying a home and not using an experiences realtor.

City vs. Suburbs. vs Rural Living

Choosing the neighborhood you would like to live in will require deciding whether you want to live in the city, suburbs or country. Many people with families usually want to live in the suburbs because there is more room for children to grow and the commute to work is still reasonable.

There are advantages to city and rural living as well. Those who live in the city will be close to work, restaurants, activities, and events. Those who live in a rural area will be able to enjoy the peace and quiet of their surroundings with less traffic and more natural beauty.

Whichever lifestyle you prefer, you should construct a pros and cons list then ranking each to determine the area best suited for your needs. The following will get you started:

City Living
  Pros
  - Easy access to cultural events
  - More restaurants and shopping
  - Public transportation
  - More people
  - More property style options such as houses, condos or apartments
  - Private and public schools

Cons
- Crime rates are higher
- Pollution
- Higher housing costs
- Higher taxes
- Higher cost of living
- Housing inventory is more limited

Country Living
Pros
- More land available
- New homes available
- Less congestion
- Cost of living is lower

Cons
- Fewer schools to choose from
- Further from restaurants and shopping
- Less of a sense of community
- Not as many cultural events
- Longer commute to work

Suburban Living
Pros
- Close to city and country
- Able to have a yard
- Cost of living is less expensive than city living
- Close to cultural events
- Community feeling

Cons
- More people in a smaller area
- Fewer schools to choose from
- Longer commute to work

When choosing the area you would like to live in, be sure to consider:
- Finances
- Schools
- Square footage of the home
- Lot size
- Taxes
- Length of commute to work

You should carefully consider all the pros/cons of city, suburban and country lifestyles. While there will always be a some less than ideal features, you should be able to find a home that will help you lead the type of lifestyle that is most important to you and your family.

Making the Commute

Most of us have a commute, to and from work, 5 days a week. Depending on where you decide to live, this could become a huge part of your day. Knowing that time is the only finite thing in life, it's important to consider how much you can devote to your work commute. While some people may be alright with an hour commute because they can listen to an audio book or their favorite morning news on the radio, you may not want to use your time this way. Unfortunately, living in the suburbs or in a country area may extend your daily commute.

If you want to remain relatively close to your job, you should not search further than a ten-mile radius. Inform your real estate agent or drive ten miles in any direction and see what is out there. Many times, there will be neighborhoods you have never heard of. You should find back roads as well as highway accessible roads that will make your commute easier.

You should also look for a home during different times of day in order to figure out the traffic patterns. If possible, consider areas that go against normal traffic patterns. That way you will not be stuck in as much traffic when going to and from work.

Schools in the Area

If you have school age children, or plan to, you will want to find a home that is close to quality schools. If you find a neighborhood that you like, find out which school district it is located in. Not all school districts are alike, and you will be sending your children to the school district your home is in unless they will enroll in private school.

While your children do not need to walk to school, being relatively close to home will make it easier to pick them up, participate in after school events, and give them a sense of community.

If the children's school is far away from your home their bus ride to and from school may take a while (like your work commute). This could take time away from getting homework done or playing with friends. Also, find out where the middle school and high schools are in the area. Eventually, your children will be attending these schools so you will want to be prepared and find out everything you can about these schools as well.

Most real estate agents will have a strong grasp on the schools in the area and will be able to provide recommendations as to which are high performing. Also, education rankings are easily accessible online and should be reviewed prior to making any home purchase. A large portion of the real estate taxes you pay are allocated towards the school systems so you will want to understand what you are paying for and the quality of education being provided there.

Grocery, Shopping and Other Necessities

While living in a country area may seem peaceful, be prepared to do a lot more driving. The nearest grocery store or pharmacy may be a considerable drive from your home. This is another factor to consider when buying your first home. While small towns have centralized areas where the shops and grocery stores are located, unless you live in town, you will have to drive in order to get there.

Many people who live in the country will adjust their lives as well as their priorities. They may go to the grocery stores once every two weeks; they will not eat at restaurants as often and will not go to the movies or other social events as often either. You will need to decide what is important to you.

Before buying a home, survey the town to see what is available. This will give you a good idea of what it would be like to live in the area. Spend a few days there if possible, to truly experience life in that town/city to see if it's a good fit.

If you are planning to stay in the city, you will have the advantages of public transportation, but you may still need a car to get to and from work or for leisure activities. While the city can be convenient in many ways, parking a car is not one of them. Many homes may have off-street parking but other homes will not. If you don't have off-street parking, you may be required to buy a street parking permit or pay monthly for a parking garage/lot space. Please note, that on-street parking may require you to move your car during snow storms which can be quite a hassle.

Other Location Considerations

- Weather
- Road conditions
- Location of property in the neighborhood

You should be thinking ahead in terms of the weather. If you are planning on living in the country, you should pay attention to possible flooding, snow, and other weather that could affect your commute. If the road is a dirt road, you should ask if the town/city will clear the road and how often they will do so. This is another advantage of living in the city because you could always use public transportation if you do not want to drive.

It's also important to ask, especially in country areas, if the road is public or private. If the road is public, that means the town/city will maintain it during the winter (salt, sand and plow) and the spring summer (street sweeping, cleaning etc.). If the road is private, the homeowners on the road will need to maintain the road and hire private companies to maintain it. Private roads should have a Private Road Maintenance Agreement to ensure every homeowner is paying their fair share, especially if there are maintenance expenses that are incurred. Consult your real estate agent for further clarification when the home you are considering is on a private road.

If the property is located at the bottom of a slope, you may have flooding issues after a rainstorm. Conversely, if your home sit up high on a hill and you have a steep driveway, you will want to consider the implications of when it snows or there is ice on the pavement. You'll need to ensure you have a vehicle capable of safely traversing this or be ready to shovel/plow and salt/sand when applicable.

There are many location considerations that you must consider. Consulting your realtor to ensure you are obtaining as much information as possible about the property will help to ensure you make the right decision.

3
Working with Realtors

Finding a real estate agent (commonly referred to as a realtor) who is looking out for your best interest is one of the most important steps to buying a home. With so much information at our fingertips, some buyers feel they can circumvent using a realtor by simply using real estate search engines online and talking with friends and family that have purchased real estate in the past. Although those can be sourced of great information, they will not replace the value added by working with a licensed real estate agent.

It's worth noting that most buyer's agents will be compensated through the commission paid by the seller. In other words, most buyers-agents do not charge <u>you</u> for their services; they are compensated, when the transaction closes, by the seller. Working with a buyers-agent will provide great information and guidance with a great price tag – *Free!*

Choosing a Realtor

There are a few ways to find a reliable realtor. For example, you can:
- Ask friends and family
- Attend a few open houses and meet realtors
- Online review sites such as Zillow, Realtor.Com or Google Business
- Walk into a local realty office
- Look for local realtors in your neighborhood by paying attention to for sale signs in the neighborhood
- **Ask me for my list of personally endorsed agents – these are agents that I have interviewed, screened, and meet my high standards!**

Asking plenty of questions when interviewing a realtor may seem like a lot of work, but when you visit a realtor for the first time, you should think about questions that will help you get to know this person who is going to help you during the process of buying your first home.

If you feel uncomfortable, then you are under no obligation to continue with this realtor. You want to find a realtor that you feel comfortable with and you create a connection with. Any realtor can show you a home but you want a realtor that you feel confident will be looking out for your interest from day 1.

You should pay attention to:
- How well they listen to your needs.
- How well they understand real estate law and contracts.
- What their online reputation is. Ask for reviews and/or research them on your own.
- How accessible are they and how willing are they to show you various properties of interest.

In the end, you will need to be the judge of the real estate agent. If they know what you are talking about, can find out information you need quickly and are willing to take the time to listen to what you need, then you should be able to work together well.

In some cases, you may be asked to sign an exclusivity agreement that states you will only work with a specific real estate agency or agent for a specified amount of time (usually 6 months). You are under no obligation to sign this agreement and you should only do so if you feel comfortable sticking with them.

While these agreements are not totally binding, it could make buying a home more difficult down the road. Only sign agreements if you feel comfortable that this agency/agent is looking out for your best interest.

During your search for a real estate agent, you will find a variety of agents that will want to work with you. These include:
- Experienced agents
- New agents
- Pushy agents
- Absentee agents
- Hard working agents

While all real estate agents have different personalities, you will have to decide which one you will want to work with when looking for your new home.

Experienced Agents vs. New Agents

This is an age-old debate that should be addressed. While an experienced agent may have sold more homes, new agents can be just as helpful and may be hungrier to make a name for themselves, which may prompt them to work harder for you.

While you should ask about their experience, you should take into consideration other traits such as willingness to listen, accessibility and local market knowledge. There is no right or wrong choice as long as your personalities mesh well together, and you feel confident they are looking out for your best interest in the transaction.

There are experienced agents out there who will drag their feet because they are overconfident, or they are too busy to provide you with the focus you need. Experienced agents may know more about different neighborhoods, but they may not be as hungry and motivated to work with a first-time buyer because they have other listings and repeat buyers to work with.

You should not let inexperience deter you when looking for an agent. Many times, new agents will work harder because they are trying to make a name for themselves and build a book of business, just as the experience agent would have done years ago.

Of course, experienced agents can be fantastic to work with as well. Just because they have plenty of experience it does not mean they will neglect you or not offer the time and effort you require. Experienced agents have been working on their craft for a while and may be the best fit for you.

Pushy Agents

Unfortunately, you will meet real estate agents who will want to sell you more than you need. To earn larger commissions or sell their listings that have been sitting on the market for a while. Many agents may "tell" you what you need instead of "ask" you what you need. This is where you will need to stand firm. You do not want to waste your time looking at homes that do not fit your budget or may require more work than you have the time, capacity or expertise to handle.

Absentee Agents

Absentee real estate agents are those agents who show you a few homes and then disappear for a few weeks. These agents may be overworked, may have just joined the industry to earn a commission check, or only work as an agent part-time and don't have the capacity to meet your needs. Whatever the reasons, this is behavior that will not be helpful to your home buying experience and should be a red flag that you need to move on.

Please note, this happens in all sorts of professions and is not unique to real estate agents. When you are working with any sales professional and they are unresponsive, hard to reach and don't give you the sense that they are working on behalf of you, moving on is likely the best next step.

Hard Working Agents

These are the best agents to help you buy your first home. If you find an agent who is diligently working for you, do not lose them. These are the agents that will follow every lead, express your wants and needs to listing agents and try their best to find you a home that meets your needs. You should expect to see some homes that they feel would be great fits and others that they may recommend you don't place an offer on. Any time a sale person is willing to convince you to not pursue a transaction that would result in them making a commission, you should recognize that as someone truly looking out for your best interest. If they only see you as a commission check, they would be pushing for you to place an offer on every home they showed you.

Now that you know more about what to look for in a real estate agent, you should feel a little more comfortable about working with one. They can be an incredible source of information for homes, neighborhoods, and other answers to questions about the communities you are looking at.

Preparing to See Homes with Your Realtor

Once you have found a realtor you are comfortable with, you will want to make the most of your time when house hunting. Giving your realtor a list of what you are looking for will help narrow the search and save everyone some time. Your list should include:
- Your price range
- Number of bedrooms
- Number of bathrooms
- Size of property

- Central heat and air conditioning requirements
- Garage
- Neighborhood
- Any other amenities you would like

Giving your real estate agent a list of your requirements/requests will allow them to create search criteria to find a home that fits (most of) your needs. You should list these amenities by importance because no home is perfect, and you'll need to figure out what is most important to you before your realtor starts their search. Let your agent know what aspects you may be flexible on and what aspects are absolute must-haves. For example, as nice as it may be to have a pool that should be much further down your must-have list than the number of bedrooms. Starting with the most important aspects, generally bedrooms/bathrooms, property type and location will help to create a realistic search model for your agent to work with.

Viewing Homes

When looking at homes with your agent, be sure to ask plenty of questions. While some questions may seem trivial, they may be important to your happiness and should not be held back. Common questions people ask their agents are:
- How old is the home?
- How many previous owners have there been?
- What kinds of renovations have been done to the home?
- How old is the plumbing?
- How old is the wiring?
- How old are the windows?
- What type of utilities does the property have?

While your agent will likely provide plenty of feedback about the property which will answer many of these questions, you should try to come up with every question you can think of that could be impactful in your decision-making process. As a first-time homebuyer, no one should expect you to be an expert homebuyer. Questions should not only be allowed, they should be encouraged.

If your agent does not know all the answers to your questions, they should be able ask questions of the listing agent, other professionals or do their own research within public records to get you the answers needed. The adage of *there is no such thing as a stupid question* is quite fitting when it comes to buying your first home.

Taking Pictures

One of the best ways to remember the homes you have seen is take pictures with your phone. Request permission from the listing agent before taking pictures but, in most cases, they will be completely open to this.

Many times, after looking at a few houses, your recollection of them may begin to overlap. You might forget how big the kitchen in home number two was in comparison to home number five. Having pictures will you evidence of the layout, finishes and other aspects that may be difficult to remember when looking at so many homes in a short period of time. This will help when you need to begin comparing the pros and cons of the homes you visited.

Narrowing Down Your Choices

After viewing multiple homes that fit your search criteria, you should be ready to narrow your choices down to a few properties. Please note, this is assuming the market is in balance between buyers and sellers. If it's a sellers-market, you may not have as much time to decide on placing a bid since inventory is likely limited and there may be multiple (quick) offers on the homes you view. But, assuming a balanced market, you should have a reasonable amount of time to consider each home carefully.

If you like a home in a neighborhood, you should ask your realtor if there are any other homes in for sale in the area and, if so, can they schedule a showing for those. Sometimes you can get hooked on an amazing neighborhood and not realize the home is overpriced or needs too much work. If, by chance, there are other homes for sale in the neighborhood it will help to compare against the property of interest. This could confirm the home is exactly what you want or, perhaps, that the home is overpriced. Having firsthand knowledge of the neighboring homes amenities, asking price etc. will help to determine the market value of the home you may offer to purchase.

If you are still not finding a home that you like, you may need to change the neighborhoods you are looking it. While this can seem disappointing, your real estate agent should be open to showing you homes in different neighborhoods. Sometimes when compare homes, you will find redeeming qualities in a home you had previously seen. Keep good notes on each property and save them along with the pictures you took. As mentioned previously, no home is going to be perfect, so you'll want to keep your options open when comparing homes.

In a sellers-market, bidding wars are common. A bidding war occurs when multiple buyers are interested in a home and they make competing offers in the hopes of *winning* the home. Bidding wars can be long, drawn out and could result in an impulse buy if too much emotion is allowed to cloud your judgment. This is not to say that entering a bidding war is a bad thing. In-fact, bidding wars generally only occur when the property is in great shape, listed at a great price or both! If you are getting into a bidding war, it's important to think rationally and not drag your feet. Bidding wars usually require a "highest and best" offer meaning you'll need to make your final offer with no expectation of back and forth price negotiations. If your offer is strong enough you have a chance to win but you need to understand there is a realistic chance you lose out and need to move on. While this can set you back, you should try to stay positive and understand that the seller is likely looking at this as a business decision and not something you should take personally.

Your agent should be there to guide you through this tense process. If you are following the steps and positioning yourself appropriately, you'll find yourself making offers confidently.

Information Realtors Should Tell You

There is plenty of information that your realtor can tell you about the homes you will be viewing. Things they should tell you include:
- The price of the home
- The age of the home
- Any renovations that have been done
- Any other issues with the home
- Property taxes
- Community dues
- Schools
- Neighborhood crime rates

You should be able to find out all the information you need to know in order to make an informed decision about buying a home with a good realtor on your side. It's important to note that realtors are required by law to give you information concerning any damage and/or repairs that they know about. This includes any incidents that have occurred inside the home such as criminal activity, fire, and other events. Furthermore, when a property is listed, the seller needs to complete a form known as the Seller Disclosures. These disclosures outline many aspects of the home that will be of interest to you such as insurance claims, age of the home, utility type/s etc. Make sure to ask for this document for all properties you are considering.

You can also do your own research on the internet or at town/city hall. You can research past events that have taken place in the neighborhood, the home itself, or the town where you want to live. I always recommend checking the tax assessor's database (all residential real estate is searchable here) to find out information about the current owner, past owner, square footage etc.

Other information realtors can provide include:
- Any recent price changes and the reason for that change. It may be because the home has been on the market for a while, but it could also be because major inspection issues have come up with a previous potential buyer. The seller knows they need to lower the price to get a new buyer interested and willing to overlook the inspection issue due to the change in price.
- Prices of other comparable sales in the area. This would be from the Comparative Market Analysis that you should request from your agent
- How quickly the owner wants or needs to sell their home
- How much are the real estate taxes and are there any exemptions such as an owner-occupied tax rate exemption.
- Are there taxes for sewer use or any other public works such as the fire district?
- What does the current owner pay for homeowners' insurance?

Working with Seller's and Buyer's Agent

As a homebuyer, your real estate agent is considered the buyer's agent. While some buyers will forego hiring an agent in the hopes of negotiating directly with the listing agent, most will end up decided to hire an agent to represent them. There is nothing wrong with working directly with the listing agent, but you need to remember that they are also looking out for the seller's best interest which could create a conflict of interest. You want an agent that will:
- Handle negotiations with the seller
- Complete paperwork

- Survey neighborhoods
- Protect your interest in the transaction

It is in your best interest to hire a buyer's agent to work on your behalf and make sure your interests are protected throughout the process.

Negotiations with Sellers

Most people who sell their home are also working with an agent. This agent is known as a seller's agent. If you choose not to hire an agent, you will be dealing with a seller's agent who is looking out for the seller's interests.

Sometimes, though, the seller's agent and the buyer's agent can be the same agent. This means that your agent is looking after the interests of everyone involved. It is best to hire a buyer's agent who can negotiate with the listing agent on your behalf so that their only focus is your interest and not the other party.

Besides negotiating with the seller on a price, initial deposit, and closing date you will want to request an inspection contingency. This means, you have a certain period (usually 10 days) to have a home inspector visit the home and look for issues with the condition of home. Quite often the home inspector will come back with a laundry list of imperfections. Ideally, the inspector will also describe the imperfection as something that requires immediate attention, something that needs monitoring or may not be an issue until years down the road. Don't be alarmed, there are always a multitude of items on the inspectors list. The important task here is to have a discussion with your inspector about the severity of each item so that you fully understand the level of concern you should have for his findings.

Once you have this list, you'll need to decide between 3 options; 1 – continue with the purchase and waive the inspection contingency, essentially agreeing the home is in the shape you expect. 2 – Go back to the seller with the list of the items that you would like to have fixed/repaired in the hopes of negotiating that work to be completed or credited off the purchase price. 3 – backout of the deal altogether if the issues are too concerning. You'll want to discuss the inspectors list with your agent as not every small issue should be requested from the seller. Normal wear and tear is to be expected when buying a lived-in home so take care to review your requests and make sure they are reasonable.

Other Reasons to Hire a Real Estate Agent

Survey Neighborhoods

Another advantage of hiring a buyer's agent is you will not need to do as much legwork to find and see homes. You will be able to request your agent find homes for sale and set up appointments on your behalf. Today, we have access to almost every home that hits the market through the various online listing sites, such as, Zillow, RedFin, Realtor.com. But your realtor may know of homes that have not hit the market but will soon be formally listed on the Multiple Listing Service (MLS). Realtors can find this information by asking around their office, by making request on social media or by various other methods. Having this information will give you a leg up on those that are simply searching the internet for listings on their own.

Peace of Mind

The bottom line is that a buyer's agent is the best resource when it comes to finding and making an offer on a home. While a seller's agent will be able to tell you the basics about a home, they are working for the seller. They will not try to get you the lowest price for the home. If you enjoy negotiating, then working with the seller's agent might be for you. But, if you are like most people, hiring an agent to work on your behalf will make the entire process more enjoyable and rewarding.

Wealth of Knowledge

Your agent should be savvy about negotiating the right price for your new home. They will be able to help you narrow down your search to find the right property and, conversely, they will be able to provide advice when walking away from a property is in your best interest. Therefore, it is so important to talk with your agent and ask as many questions as you can before buying a home.

Confidence

If you are having doubts about purchasing the home, after making an offer, you should tell your agent right away so they can prevent you from going any further in the transaction, hopefully preventing you from losing any deposits or third party expenses. Many times, the initial shock of being a homeowner can be overwhelming. Sometimes talking with your agent is enough to resolve your feelings. Other times, you may need to see a few more homes before deciding. Your agent will be able to give you practical advice during this time and should be thought of as a trusted advisor.

4
Playing the Housing Market: Buying vs. Renting

Understanding the dynamics of the real estate market will put you in a better position when preparing to buy a home. There are times when it's a buyers-market and other times when it's a seller-market; There are times when real estate values are appreciating quickly and other times when values are decreasing. Furthermore, there are times when its beneficial to be a homeowner while other times when renting is the best option. Unless you are a seasoned real estate investor it is unlikely you'll be able to truly master the real estate market but having a strong foundation and understanding of real estate market dynamics is a must when considering home ownership.

Watching the Housing Market

For the last decade we have seen housing prices increase rather dramatically. As we left the great recession, the housing market was in shambles and, as such, home values had dropped considerably. For those that had the liquidity and risk-tolerance, this was an AMAZING time to buy real estate. As more and more buyers re-entered the market the value of homes started increasing. The first few years of this economic recovery were considered a buyer's market because sellers were desperate to sell and there was a plethora of homes for sale, generally at depressed prices. This dynamic coupled with a recovering jobs market and a steady decrease in mortgage interest rates started to shift the industry into a seller's market. In this seller's market, less and less homes were on the market because sellers were enjoying their home appreciation and didn't want to miss out on additional appreciation down the road. Further exacerbating the issue was those sellers having difficulty locating a suitable move-up home because of the tight inventory at the high-end of the market.

It's inevitable that the market will flip back to a buyers-market at some point. It's simple supply-demand economics. Knowing when that will occur is impossible, even for an industry professional, so trying to time the market as a first-time homebuyer shouldn't be on your homebuying preparation list. Instead, it's important to understand the dynamic relationship between supply, demand and real estate prices when considering a home purchase.

While you should not be losing sleep over the housing market, you should keep the following in mind before buying your first home:
- The historic market valuation of the home and neighborhood you are considering
- How does your budget match up with this home? Are you stretching yourself or is this a home you will grow out of too quickly?
- What are the housing value projections for the neighborhood?
- Are property listings experiencing price reductions or are they selling for full price?

When buying a home, you want to do your best to ensure it's a sound financial decision. Over the long term its probable the property will increase in value, but, it's very difficult to time the market in a way that allows for you to only see appreciation and not experience depreciation. Buying real estate is similar to buying a stock when looked at through a financial lense; there is an offer price (list price) and a bid price (your offered amount) and an eventual execution price (agreed upon sales price). The market will continue to fluctuate during your time as the homeowner. Hopefully, the market works in your favor and you can sell the property for a profit down the road but that is not always the case.

Although property and a stock have similarities, there is one very stark difference; you and your family will be occupying the home whereas a stock is simply an asset held in your portfolio. A home offers shelter, it can be the location of holiday parties and will be a place in which memories are created. Stocks can't be valued in the same way as a home because of the emotional attachment that comes along with homeownership.

Making the Most of the Housing Market

There are many variables in the housing market and having a high-level awareness of them will be helpful to develop your understanding of real estate.

Interest Rates for Mortgages

Interest rates are an important consideration when purchasing real estate. The higher your interest rate is, the larger your monthly mortgage payment will be which will result in less house you can afford. When property values are low, paying a higher interest rate is not as burdensome because you're paying a higher percentage of a smaller amount. In other words, paying 8% on a $100,000 mortgage is more manageable than 5% on a $500,000 mortgage. Of course, we would all prefer the lowest rate possible but understanding that interest rates are relative to the amount borrowed is quite important.

Currently, we are in a market in which interest rates have never been lower. We've seen a steady decline in mortgage rates since in the 1980's when mortgage rates were in the 16-18% range. As these rates fell, we saw homes appreciate rather quickly. It's not unreasonable for a home that was purchased in 1980 for $30,000 to be work $250,000 in our current market. A big reason behind this is the steady decrease in interest rates which allowed more consumers access to higher credit limits which fueled demand and in-turn increased property values. Of course, there are plenty of other factors that contributed to this value appreciation, but interest rates certainly played a major role.

We are in uncharted territory with the market interests being what they are now a days. We've never seen interest rates so low and home prices so high. This is not to say we are about to fall off of a cliff or that we are in for an unprecedented collapse of the market but instead that it's very difficult to predict what the market will look like 1, 5 or 10 years from now.

Understanding how interest rates impact you and your potential home purchase is very important when deciding to become a homeowner. Some of the factors that will be considered by your lender when quoting you an interest rate will be:

- The other types of debt you currently have
- Current credit scores
- Credit history, specifically, timeliness of payments made
- Number of credit cards and the utilization rate of each
- Type of property (single family, multi-family, condo etc.)
- Down payment
- Loan type

Building Rates in Your Area

Housing inventory is an important determinant of housing prices and the health of the real estate market. The only ways to increase the supply of available real estate is either to have more current owners list their homes or builders to build new homes. Building new homes usually attracts higher-end buyers since most new builds are priced higher than that of existing homes. This is partially because the builders are looking to increase their profit margins but also because new homes can include new technologies such as smart-home devices or other amenities that may not have been around before. Another growing trend in new homes are larger garages. As the US consumer opts to purchase SUVs and trucks over sedans, older garages are being squeezed for every inch they have.

You'll notice that areas with new construction begin to increase in value. Existing homes experience this appreciation as well because those new larger homes can pull up the value of the existing housing stock. For example, if a new development is being built with 10 new $400K-500K homes, in an area that currently contains homes valued around $325-400K, you'll see those existing home values start to appreciate. This is because some buyers may not be able to afford those higher price points, but they like the area and will expand their search criteria to homes that are a bit older. They will likely have access to some additional capital so they will be able to renovate the existing home and increase the market value. When this occurs on a large scale, the entire neighborhood and surrounding areas see price appreciation. Area that are experiencing an uptick in building generally experience more rapid price appreciation as well.

Foreclosures in Your Area

A foreclosure is the process in which a lender re-takes possession of a property due to non-payment or various other reasons that would have been outlined as events of repossession in the Mortgage contract. In Rhode Island, foreclosures are non-judicial meaning the lender does not need to go to court in order to start foreclosure proceedings.

Foreclosures can have a significant impact on the real estate market for a few reasons. First, homes that are being (or were) foreclosed are likely not well maintained and are generally sold at a steep discount because of the condition. This sale price is noted as public record and when another similar home is sold in the area, that foreclosure could be considered as a "comparable sale" on the appraisal. It will likely be noted as a foreclosure on the appraisal but, regardless, if a home with the same lot size, same number of beds/baths and same squared footage is sold at foreclosure for 20% below market value, it will have an impact on your appraised value. Secondly, foreclosures have a negative impact on the surrounding area because they degrade the neighborhood and can deter potential buyers from wanting to live near a home that may be in disrepair, abandoned or otherwise neglected.

This is not to say that a foreclosure should be completely disregarded as a potential property to purchase. Many foreclosures can be rehabilitated rather easily and can be purchased for a competitive price. It is important to understand how foreclosures can impact the surrounding areas when looking in neighborhoods that have experienced foreclosures in the past.

Buying vs. Renting

If you will own the home for a long period of time, buying is more cost effective than renting. If history is an indicator of the future, home values will appreciate over time. This compounded appreciation will generally more than offset the higher cost of buying rather than to rent. But that is not to say everyone should buy a home during their lifetime. For some, renting makes the most sense. Some may prefer the mobility of not being tied to any specific area which can be rewarding when their work has them relocate often. Others may not want to deal with the constant upkeep of owning a home. While others may not have the financial means to buy a home. If buying a home and maintaining it will create a budget that is unsustainable for you then you should reconsider buying. Having a conversation with your financial advisor should help to outline

There are plenty of pros and cons when it comes to buying a home compared to renting a home. Since you are thinking about buying your first home, you should consider the following:

Buying a Home
  Pros
  - Investment property – Possible tax advantages (seek professional advice regarding tax considerations)
  - Build equity and home appreciation
  - Almost any home improvements can be completed at your discretion
  - You do not need to answer to a landlord
  - Sense of stability

Cons

- You are responsible for all repair and maintenance costs
- Monthly payments for utilities and mortgage are usually more expensive than rent
- Lack of mobility. It could take time to sell the property

Renting a Home
Pros

- You are not responsible for repairs and maintenance costs
- You are free to leave once the lease has expired
- In many cases, utilities are paid by the landlord
- Many apartment buildings have security systems
- Rental payments are usually less than a mortgage payment
- Credit isn't impacted by missed rent payments

Cons

- Privacy issues
- May need to share washers and dryers
- Rent can be increased once lease expires
- Landlords are not always reliable
- Decorating/renovations may need landlord approval
- Deposit may be required
- Restrictions on pets
- Can't build equity

Rent to Own

Another option you may have is to buy the property you are currently renting or rent a property that also offers you the option to buy after a certain amount of time. This will give you a chance to see if you like living in the home and will give you time to get your finances in order.

Rent to own properties are usually older than other homes and have been rental properties for some time. This means that they may not be in great shape. If you are looking for a property that you don't mind repairing, then this option may be for you.

When looking for a rent to own property, you should ask the following questions:

- How old is the home?
- How many times has it been rented out?

- What is the mortgage payment on the home?
- What is the rent per month for the home?
- How long will I have to make my decision?
- What happens if I change my mind?

If you are going to pursue a rent to own property, you should have the property contracts drafted and executed by you and the landlord to ensure no surprises arise. This will protect your rights and the rights of the seller/landlord. Many times, a portion of the monthly rental payment can be considered towards the down payment requirement. In other words, if you agreed to pay $1,200/mo. in rent, you could agree that $200/mo., of that payment, will go towards the purchase price and/or down payment. If this is something you are considering, you should consult with a loan officer to ensure you document this properly. This will help to avoid issues when you are ready to pursue the home purchase.

Using the Housing Market to Your Advantage

By paying attention to the current housing trends and keeping an eye on homes in your area, you will be able to make an informed offer, increasing the likelihood of be accepted.

When watching the housing market, consider the following:
- The number of homes for sale in your area (inventory)
- The number of days homes are on the market before selling (days on market)
- The price of a new home compared to an existing home, usually expressed in dollars per square foot (price per sq. foot)
- Current market interest rates and their trending direction
- The time of year

Springtime is a good time to buy a home for several reasons:
- More people want to sell
- It is easier to make appointments to view homes
- Weather is better; during the winter months snow may prevent you from inspecting every aspect of the home
- Income tax returns can help down payment and closing costs

There will be plenty of people who could not sell their homes in the fall or winter months and who are planning to list in late-winter or early spring. This increase in inventory usually allows for buyers to get some good deals as sellers are competing with other sellers to get their home sold at the same time and may be willing to negotiate a bit.

While there is not a best time to buy a home, the spring is generally considered the start of the real estate buying market. Depending on how much time you have to work with, monitoring the market during all 4 seasons will generate varying results. In other words, some sellers may think selling in the winter months is more difficult, so they feel they need to offer their home at a reduced price. Whether this is true or not, paying attention to housing trends/prices throughout all four seasons, can potentially lead to great deals in the real estate market.

In the End

In the end, when you are ready to buy a home, you should make the decision based on what works for your budget. Finding a great deal on a home in the perfect neighborhood only makes sense if it's the right time for you. Understanding the underlying economics of real estate is important when making your real estate decisions and needs to be understood before you begin your home search. You also need to consider your financial position and if you are comfortable being a homeowner. As mentioned earlier, not everyone is destined to be a homeowner and there is nothing wrong with that.

Becoming a homeowner is a personal decision and one that takes considerable thought, research and preparation. If you are unsure about whether you are ready to buy a home, speak to friends/family and listen to their feedback. It also is a good idea to contact your financial advisor and your loan officer to review the numbers with them. Sometimes you can become concerned that a mortgage is too expensive for you to afford but after reviewing the numbers, it's not as concerning as you once thought.

"By failing to prepare you are preparing to fail."

5
Home Inspections

A home inspection is conducted by a licensed professional who inspects as many aspects of the home as deemed necessary to determine what issues, if any, there are with the property. Ask your realtor for a recommendation of someone they trust to conduct this inspection.

The Importance of Home Inspections

Finding a home does not mean that your investigative duties are over. Although most states do not have required inspections, your lender may require certain inspections based upon the type of loan you have applied for. For example, veterans loans (VA) require a pest inspection and a well inspection (assuming the property isn't hooked into public water). If there are termites or other insects, the homeowners will have to take care of the problem before they sell the home. If the well has contaminants (usually lead, coliform or nitrates) a treatment system will need to be installed.

But what about full home inspections? Are they worth it? In most cases, the answer is yes. Although most home inspections can cost between $300-$1,000, it may save you a lot of money in the long run.

A thorough home inspection will include checking the following:

- Electrical systems
- Heating and cooling systems
- Foundation
- Siding
- Structural elements
- Roof
- Insulation
- Doors and windows
- Plumbing

If you are buying a new or used home, you will generally have an inspection contingency built into the contract. The normal time frame is 10 days (this could vary for new construction). Once the inspection report comes back, you will have the opportunity to review the inspector's findings and determine if you want to ask for repairs, a price reduction or move forward as-is.

It is common for buyers of older homes to request repairs and/or a price reduction from the seller, but common sense is warranted when asking for these repairs. Every home is going to have some normal wear and tear and it's not realistic to expect a seller to restore a home to its as-new condition, unless you are paying top dollar for the home.

When drawing up the initial offer to purchase the home, your agent should include language that outlines an inspection period and allows you to cancel the contract, including the return of the deposit monies, if the inspection is not satisfactory.

How to Find a Home Inspector

There are a few places to turn when looking for a home inspector:
- Your real estate agent
- Your loan officer
- References from friends and family

Your real estate agent should be the first person you ask for a home inspector reference. Usually, they will only work with 1 or 2 different inspectors because they know and trust these folks. The home inspector and agent should have a strong working relationship and if you are trusting of your agent, you should be able to trust their referrals as well.

But, if you would like to shop around for a home inspector or are getting a referral from a friend/family, there are some questions you should ask them to confirm their level of expertise:
- How long have you been inspecting homes?
- How much do you charge?
- What type of inspections do you offer? Some inspectors have specialized inspections they can offer such as radon, inground pool and private well.
- What is your availability? You will want a full-time inspector, not someone that does this as a side-gig.

Once you have asked these questions, find out if your lender has specific inspections that the home must pass before your loan can be approved. If the inspector can complete these inspections along with the home inspection, then you should request these all be completed during the same time frame. This will cut down on cost and help to keep the process moving quickly.

What to Expect from a Home Inspection

A home inspection can reveal many problems you did not notice during the open house or subsequent visits to the property. Some inspection items that may be present include:

- Crumbling/cracking foundation
- Structural damage to floors, walls and ceilings
- Water damage inside and outside of the walls
- Termite damage
- Porch railings or posts in poor condition
- Heating and cooling systems need to be cleaned or do not work properly
- Roof needs repair
- Broken or leaking pipes
- Electrical system issues including improper/unsafe wiring
- Broken water fixtures or light fixtures
- Windows that do not open
- Uneven doorways
- Improper insulation
- Mold
- Septic tank failure

Most homes will only experience a few minor issues, but some older homes may have more problems. The issues with the home could cost you thousands of dollars if you are unaware of the damage prior to purchasing the home. While disclosure of some problems is mandatory, many homeowners do not even know that other problems exist because they have not had an inspection since they purchased the home many years ago.

On the day of the inspection, you should expect to receive a detailed report of the inspector's findings. This report will outline the various items that were inspected, and they will usually be given a rating of either needs repair, monitor and/or satisfactory. Depending on the rating the inspector may further explain what steps should be taken to remedy the issue.

Specific Places that Should be Inspected

When interviewing home inspectors, make sure to ask whether the following areas are inspected:

- Chimney and fireplace
- Attic and basement
- Crawl space

- Swimming pools
- Smoke detectors and appliances

These are important and can be very costly to repair. Many sellers are willing to address major concerns when they are brought to their attention by a buyer from the home inspection. The reasoning is that almost every buyer is going to have a home inspection and if it's likely the next inspector will have the same concern; they might as well take care of it now.

Chimney and Fireplace
- Missing, broken, or intact chimney caps
- Mortar between chimneys is intact
- Metal chimneys are not bent or contain holes and have all screws in place
- Presence of creosote – this is buildup caused from wood burning fireplaces, and is flammable if not removed

Attic, Basement, and Crawl Spaces
- Mold
- Fire damage
- Rotting beams
- Insulation
- Damage from water
- Damage from animals and pests

Swimming Pools
- Pool plumbing including pipes, pump and filter
- Pool lining
- Pool cover

Smoke Detectors and Appliances
- Test alarm
- Check for broken hoses or connections
- Broken door handles
- Improper wiring

Pest Inspection

A pest inspection is a separate inspection that will give you an idea of structural damage to the home that has been caused by termites and other pests/insects. If you are applying for a VA loan or the appraiser notes pest damage/infestation (for any loan type) you will need this inspection completed prior to closing.

Termite inspections are not covered under the standard fee of a home inspection, so this will likely be an additional fee on top of the standard home inspection cost.

The inspection should take about 1 hour, depending on the size of the home. The inspector will look underneath the siding, in basements, attics, and around the foundation of the home to see if there are termites, ants, beetles or any another pest present. The inspector will also conduct an inspection inside the home.

Termites can be removed using an insecticide that is specially designed to kill termites and their eggs, but the damage left behind can be considerable. If the home has been infested for a long time, then it may be beyond repair.

If the damage from the pests appears to be extensive, you should consider walking away from this home. An inspector will usually be able to identify the presence of the pest and point out areas in which they are (or were) present but they can't realistically check every post and beam in the home. Sometimes a second opinion or having a contractor visit the home to provide a quote for repairs can provide some sense of the damage beyond what an inspection report may show.

How the Seller Will React

How the seller will react to the results of the home inspection could determine whether you continue pursuing the home or whether you walk away.

Sellers have their own agenda when it comes to selling their home. These could include:
- Buying another home
- Moving to another state
- Using the money to pay for family medical emergencies
- Retirement
- Profiting from the sale

This means that there are varying degrees as to what they are willing to pay for and what they are not willing to pay for. If the seller is not in a rush to sell, then they may contest the findings and refuse to repair certain items. Conversely, they may be willing to repair some items but not everything. Hopefully they are not reluctant to repair anything, and usually this isn't the case, especially if the lender is unable to approve the loan given the condition of the property. All that being said, this is a negotiation and they have the right to respond to your request as they so choose.

You will have to make some tough decisions at this point. If the repairs will be needed on the home are required by the lender, you can:
- Try to get the seller to pay for the repairs
- Pay for the repairs yourself
- Discuss different loan options with your lender to see if there are programs that won't require the work be completed prior to closing
- Walk away from the home

As in any negotiations, it's important to understand the seller's position. For example, if the seller has already moved and the subject property is vacant and waiting to be sold, the seller may be more open to dropping the price to sell the home. If they have another home with a mortgage on it, they may want (or need) to get rid of this property ASAP for cash flow reasons. You can use this type of information to your advantage if you are able to ascertain it during the showing or at the open house. Ask questions and gain as much knowledge as you can about the owners and the property to ensure your position to negotiate from is strong.

Ways a Home Inspection Can Lower the Final Price

Even though the cost of a home inspection can be rather expensive, usually totaling between $300 - $1,000, the potential savings can more than offset the cost. There are three main ways to utilize the home inspection to save money or add value to your side of the transaction.

Ask the seller to make repairs
This is the best way to save money on your new home. While you will not see a reduction in the final price of the home, you will have less work to do after moving in which will save you money and time.
Having the work completed by the seller prior to your purchase will ensure additional issues/costs that arise will be covered by the seller. You'll want to ask the seller to keep the receipts/invoices so you can document the

work and you may even want to ask if you could have your contractor do the work if you feel as though the craftsmanship may be subpar otherwise. If you have work completed after your home inspection, you'll want to make sure this work is completed prior to closing. Depending on the scope of the work, your lender's appraiser may need to revisit the home to confirm the work was completed, this is called a final appraisal inspection. This is important to get scheduled as soon as possible to ensure the closing does not get delayed.

Ask the seller for a price reduction

If the seller does not want to spend money on the repairs, they may agree to drop the sales price.

If the homeowners suggest a reduction in the final price, you should consider the offer and find out how much the repairs will cost you. If it seems like a fair deal, then take it. If not, you can always ask for a larger reduction. If you decide to pursue a price reduction strategy, it is important to provide evidence to support the amount of the reduction. You have a much greater chance of having the seller accept your offer when you provide invoices/quotes to show how much the work would cost. If you request an arbitrary amount without any back-up to explain why, the seller may be reluctant to accept.

Please note, although you may be happy with the price reduction in lieu of the work being completed, your lender may not. Your lender wants to ensure the property they are securing their loan against is in good condition. If they feel as though the required repairs are necessary prior to close, you may not have the option of a price reduction.

Ask the seller to pay for all closing costs

Another way to save money without relying on the seller to pay for the repairs is if they agree to pay your closing costs.

There are various closing costs and prepaid items (explained in detailed a bit later) that the buyer is responsible to pay at closing on top of the down payment. It is common for the seller to cover this cost in the form of a seller concession or seller closing cost credit. This can be used to offset the amount of cash you need to bring to closing which will allow you to allocate those funds for the required repairs. The seller would net less money from their sales price because of this credit but if it allows them to forgo your repair list, they may be open to the idea.

Any agreements that you make with the homeowners should be made in writing. Verbal agreements are much more difficult to argue in court and are not common practice among real estate lawyers and agents when they are closing a deal. Your agent should have a Purchase and Sales

Addendum that can outline the credit and any applicable changes and should be signed by both buyer and seller.

The Final Walkthrough

On the day of the closing, you should have a final walkthrough whether you are purchasing a new home or an older home. Final walkthroughs are a way for you to determine if there is anything else you will need to discuss, get in writing, or have changed before you sign the paperwork.

Here is what you should be checking during your final walkthrough:

- Making sure all repair requests are complete
- Central A/C is working (if 65 degrees or warmer)
- Confirm gas/oil heat is working
- Water is on and running (flush toilets and run sinks/showers)
- Garage door opener is functioning
- Test doors and windows
- All appliances that were remaining are still in the home
- Appliances are in good working condition
- Electrical systems are working
- Turn on all lights
- All junk is removed from the yard as per prior agreements

The seller should have emptied the home and it should be in broom-swept condition. If there are any issues with the home, you'll want to bring these to the attention of your realtor as soon as possible. It is not common, but it can happen in which something goes wrong during the walk-through and it's important that any issues get addressed as soon as possible.

6
Financing Your First Home

Financing your first home can be the most time-consuming part of the home buying process. There are plenty of documents that need to be signed, various other documents you'll need to provide to evidence your income, assets, liabilities and credit along with a carefully orchestrated group of third parties (closing attorney, homeowners insurance agent, appraisers etc.) that need to be involved with obtaining a mortgage. This can be difficult and frustrating to many buyers. But, as we've mentioned throughout this book, if you prepare properly and align yourself with professionals, this process can go smoothly and with little to no headaches.

It's important to have a basic understanding of the different mortgage terms, types and requirements before applying for a home loan.

Types of Home Loans

Conventional

A conventional mortgage usually has more rigorous requirements to qualify for but also has more favorable terms than most other types of loans. Lenders that offer conventional mortgages usually follow Fannie Mae or Freddie Mac, two Government Sponsored Entities (GSEs), guidelines. Fannie Mae and Freddie Macs role in the mortgage market is to add liquidity by securing loans written by lenders across the country. Since these entities back so many loans, the guidelines are uniform between almost all lenders that offer conventional financing.

Conventional financing is usually thought of as suitable for a borrower with 20% down, a credit score of 740+ and a stable employment history but this is not always the case. Conventional financing will allow borrowers with lower credit scores (usually down to 620) and lesser down payment (as little as 3%) if they have compensating factors such as a very low debt-to-income ratio, ample liquid reserves etc. Many buyers can meet the requirements of the conventional financing and are able to secure favorable terms because of it.

FHA

FHA stands for Federal Housing Authority and is a loan that is insured, by the FHA, in the event of default. Because lenders have this added layer of security, the guidelines are less rigorous than a conventional loan. Most lenders have guidelines that allow for credit scores as low as 580, down payments as low as 3.5% and credit events such as a recent bankruptcy and/or foreclosure.

FHA allows for these looser regulations by requiring all borrowers to pay an up-front mortgage insurance premium (UFMIP) and monthly mortgage insurance premiums (MIP). As of the writing of this book, the UFMIP is 1.75% and the MIP is .85% of the base loan amount. These insurance premiums are collected by FHA and used whenever a borrower defaults on this type of loan for insurance payouts.

FHA is a very common loan for a first-time buyer because of the small down payment required (3.5%) and the relaxed guidelines. First time buyers may not have had time to save up for a large down payment or may have less than perfect credit which is why this product has become so popular in the mortgage market today.

VA

A VA mortgage is a loan guaranteed the Department of Veteran Affairs. This loan is only available for the men and women of the armed services that have either served (or are serving) as an active duty member or a reservist.

A VA loan allows for the borrower to finance up to 100% of the purchase price with favorable terms and without the need for mortgage insurance. Except for a few specific scenarios, this loan requires the veteran to pay a VA Funding Fee. The amount of the funding fee depends on many factors such as active duty vs. reservist, first time or subsequent use etc.

The guidelines for VA loans are much more relaxed than conventional financing and usually less expensive than FHA financing which is why this product is so popular for veterans. The VA understands the sacrifices our veterans have endured to protect the freedoms we enjoy every day so they thought it only right to offer a mortgage product to assist with veterans homeownership in a way that would be less costly than some other programs.

USDA
A USDA mortgage is backed by the United States Department of Agriculture. The purpose of this product is to promote affordable homeownership for low to moderate income households in rural areas. Unlike conventional, FHA and VA loans, a USDA loan requires the property be in targeted areas that are deemed to be rural. Furthermore, there are certain income limitations to this program to prevent borrowers who may be able to qualify for other types of loans from using this program. Many buyers would like to use a USDA loan because it allows them to finance100% of the purchase price but the income restrictions cap the potential buyers who can be approved so that those they are trying to target with the program are the ones utilizing it.

There is a considerable amount of Rhode Island that is considered, by the USDA, as rural territory. There are tools online that you can use to search for specific properties to determine property eligibility. Always consult with your loan officer to confirm whether the property is considered rural by the USDA.

Portfolio
Portfolio mortgages are loans that lenders keep on their books and are not sold in the secondary mortgage market. This type of loan is most commonly offered by local banks and credit unions as an outlet for loans that may not be suitable as a conventional, FHA, VA or USDA loan. For example, many home construction loans are kept as portfolio loans by local banks and credit unions. Although conventional financing does allow for construction loans, it can sometimes be easier for a local lender to offer this product because they can create their own underwriting rules which may be suitable for complex loan scenarios.

Another reason for portfolio loans is that some borrowers may have a great financial profile except for one small thing that prohibits them from qualifying for standard loan options. For example, if a buyer is looking to purchase a condo in a development that has a high concentration of investors (properties used as rental properties), most lenders are unable to offer financing to this borrower with the exception of some portfolio lenders. The portfolio lender will usually charge a higher rate for the added risk of the property but it will allow the transaction to occur so it can often be a worthwhile loan type.

Unique/Specialized Loans
There are other loan types that are not as common such as a home equity line of credit (HELOC), a reverse mortgage (HECM), hard money loan etc. These loans all have their purpose and role in the mortgage market but are not discussed here since they are usually not suitable for a first-time home buyer. For further information on these unique loan products you should consult with your loan officer.

Fixed vs. Adjustable Rate Options
It is very important to understand not only the difference between fixed and adjustable rate mortgages but also why you would choose one over the other.

An adjustable rate mortgage or ARM is a loan that is fixed for a specified period, usually 5, 7 or 10 years then the rate adjusts each year thereafter for the remaining life of the loan. The reason a buyer would select an adjustable rate is if they know, with a strong degree of certainty, that they will only keep the home (or loan) for a time period less than the fixed rate term. For example, if you applied or a 7/1 ARM, the rate would be fixed for the first 7 years with an adjustment in each 1-year period after that, usually up to the standard 30-year term. If the buyer knows they will only live in the home for 6 years at most, the adjustment periods would never come into play because the loan would be paid off by then. Many times, adjustable rates carry a lower interest rate than a fixed rate loan because the lender doesn't need to guarantee the rate for as long. If the rate is lower and you know you won't keep the loan longer than the locked in period, an adjustable rate may be suitable.

A fixed rate mortgage is self-explanatory; the rate for the entire term of the loan will not change. The benefit to a fixed rate mortgage is you have a defined principal and interest payment for the entire life of the loan. Fixed rate loans are significantly more popular than adjustable because of the dependability and knowledge that the rate will never increase. It is almost always recommended that first time buyers apply for a fixed rate because of the certainty and security it offers. The 30-year fixed is the gold standard by which all of loans terms are compared and is almost always the best option for someone buying their first home.

Jumbo Loans
A jumbo loan has a balance that is greater than the conforming loan limit which is set annually by the Federal Housing Finance Agency (FHFA). FHFA reviews property value appreciation and sets a limit to the loan

amount that Fannie Mae and/or Freddie Mac will secure. As of Jan 1, 2020, this limit is being raised from $484,350 to $510,400. Any loan that is $510,401 or more is considered a jumbo loan.

Jumbo mortgages have stricter guidelines and can be more difficult to qualify for than a conventional loan. Some areas, such as San Francisco and Hawaii, are considered high-cost and have a higher limit of $765,600. This is to allow buyers in more expensive parts of the country to be have similar access to financing even though home prices are far greater.

Required Documentation

When you are going through the preapproval process or while you are applying for a mortgage, your lender will request quite a few financial documents to confirm your income, assets, credit etc. The list will usually consist of:

- 2 years of personal and business tax returns (all pages)
- 2 years of W2/1099s
- 2 most recent paycheck stub
- 2 months of bank statements (all pages)
    - With explanations of any large deposits
- 2 recent 401K statements (if applicable) all pages
- Mortgage statement, property tax bill, homeowner's insurance and association/condo fee statement for all real estate owned
- License/Identification
- Credit explanation letter

You will be asked additional questions that will help the lenders determine if you are able to pay the loan back on time. These questions include:

- Last 2 years of residency (address, length of occupancy, ownership/rental etc.)
- How long have you been at your current job?
- Are you a salaried, commissioned or hourly employee?
- Do you have any additional income from social security, rents etc.?
- How many dependents do you have?

There are plenty more questions that will be asked that cover your employment, assets, credit (current and previous), marital status, real estate ownership etc. Be prepared to provide this information so that the loan officer can properly document everything as soon as possible.

The preapproval process can seem overwhelming, but it is always best to be up-front and transparent with your loan officer. Remember, your loan officer is looking for the best product to fits your needs and qualifications so the more detail you can provide up-front, the quicker the loan officer can provide a recommendation. Withholding information about a bankruptcy or something else that you think could hurt your chances will likely only create issues further along in the process when the issue eventually surfaces.

What Not to do When Applying for a Home Loan

There are a few things you should not do when you've applied (or will be applying) for a mortgage:

- Apply for a new loan, including a credit card, personal loan or vehicle loan
- Leave your current employer
- Make any large purchase on credit or with your liquid assets
- Miss payments on your current debts

Any change to your employment, credit or assets can have a significant impact on the decision to approve or deny your mortgage. Buying a new car could increase your debt-to-income ratio; leaving your employer may render your income ineligible for qualifying purposes; missing a payment could drop your credit scores increasing the rate you qualify for or, worse, making your credit profile unacceptable for the loan you've applied for.

If you must make any purchase or do something that will change your credit profile prior to closing on the loan, consult your loan officer prior to executing any changes. Your loan officer may be able to walk you through steps to take to allow for the change, inform you of what paperwork may be needed to support it or recommend alternative steps altogether.

Don't forget, your loan officer is on your side and should be acting as your advocate throughout the process. Work closely with them and be completely open and honest even if you feel your deal could be in jeopardy. Most seasoned loan officers have experience working through complex issues and should be able to provide valuable guidance.

Amount I can Afford vs. Amount I am Approved For

How much you can afford and how much you can be approved for sound very similar but are almost always quite different. How much you can afford is a question only you (and possibly your financial advisor) can answer whereas how much you can be approved for is something your loan officer can answer and, usually, the answers are much different.

To determine how much you can afford you should create a budget like the one on the follow page. This will provide a breakdown of the income you have coming in, the expenses you have going out and how much is left over at the end. Once you've outlined this budget, you will be able to properly answer how much you can afford. If you complete this budget and you realize that you don't have any extra money left over each month, that means you are already at your max housing payment (or perhaps you've even surpassed it). If you find that you have money left over after paying bills, living expenses and allocating for savings, then you can add that left over money to the amount you are paying in rent to determine how much you can afford each month.

How much you can get approved for is similar in that your lender compares your expenses (car, credit cards, student loans, housing) versus your income but differs in that they do not take into consideration your expenses for entertainment, savings etc. In other words, a lender may inform you that you are approved with a housing payment of $2,000/mo. BUT if you are currently paying $1,500/mo. and struggling to make ends meet then there is a considerable difference in your definition of affordability and the lenders definition of approvability.

Having a budget available for your loan officer will allow them to quickly formulate a price range for your home search and help set expectations quickly for all involved.

BUDGET

INCOME	AMOUNT
Borrower Gross Income	
Co-Borrower Gross Income	
TOTAL GROSS INCOME	
NET INCOME (take home)	

EXPENSES	AMOUNT
Rent	
Food	
Utilities (gas, water, electric, trash)	
Home Maintenance	
Vehicle (car payment, insurance, gas, etc.)	
Cell Phone	
Child Care	
Credit Card Payments	
Miscellaneous	
TOTAL EXPENSES	

NET INCOME	
TOTAL EXPENSES	
MONTHLY SURPLUS OR SHORTAGE	

Increase Your Chance of Approval

There are steps you can take to help your chance of being approved for your mortgage. These steps are important to sound financial management and should be followed regardless of buying a home.

Financial Check-Up and/or consultation

Let's face it, life can become hectic and time is a scarce commodity. Many of us do not get home from work and think "let me review my finances and ensure my income and expenses are in order." We usually only begin to inspect our finances when we have a big purchase, such as a home, on the horizon. We should all try to review our finances at least 1 time per month to make sure we have money going towards savings, retirement and that our bills are being paid timely.

For those that do not have the time or expertise to properly plan and budget, hiring a financial advisor may be in your best interest. Most financial advisors will work with you to create a budget, financial goals and provide a detailed analysis of areas for improvement.

For many first-time home buyers, financial literacy is not something that was taught at any level of primary, secondary or higher education yet you are expected to enter the work force and be able to be financially literate. This is failure on the part of the education system, but it is unfortunately the system we have in place and we need to find solutions to deal with it.

Mortgage literacy is a sub-set of financial literacy and is something that is even less likely to be discussed in most education platforms. For this reason, it's important to meet with a loan officer, well in advance of purchasing your first home, to gain the knowledge needed to make an informed decision about how and when to purchase real estate. It's possible your finances are in order and you are ready to make a purchase after your initial consultation with your loan officer (which is great!) but if you have areas that need improvement, it could require months (or years) to clean up your financial profile.

Managing credit card debt

It's important to manage debt, especially when considering the purchase of a new home. Credit cards can play a significant role in the mortgage qualification process including the programs you may qualify for and the interest rate you'll be paying. Preparing for your home purchase by limiting, or ideally eliminating, credit card debt is a wise decision.

Paying bills on time
Part of the focus of your monthly budget should be monitoring your monthly expenditures. Housing, vehicle, student loans, credit cards payments etc. are usually all reported to the credit bureau and can have an impact, good or bad, on your credit profile. In most cases, the credit bureaus are not notified of a late payment until you are 30+ days late but it's important to make payments by the due dates to avoid blemishes on your credit and late fees. Missing a small credit card payment by 30+ days could be the difference between qualifying and not qualifying for a mortgage. Many banks/credit unions offer bill pay services that allow for automatic payments of these debts. This can be a great tool for those that may be less detail oriented and have limited time to manage their budget.

What Makes Up My Credit Score

Credit scores and the formulas that the three major credit bureaus use are a closely guarded secret. However, in general here are the five major areas that agencies consider when determining your score.

Payment History-35%
The most important component of your credit score is the timeliness of your payment history. This component considers the following factors:
- Have you paid your bills on time? Paying bills more than 30 days late has a negative impact on your score.
- If you've paid late, how late were you – 30 days, 60 days, or 90+ days? The later you are, the worse it is for your score.
- Have any of your accounts gone to collections? This is a red flag to potential lenders that you do not manage your debts well.
- Do you have any charge offs, debt settlements, bankruptcies, foreclosures, lawsuits, wage attachments, liens or judgments against you? These are considered significant derogatory credit events and may require you to wait before any lender will approve you for a loan. For example, if you filed a Chapter 7 bankruptcy, conventional lending guidelines require you to wait 4 years, from the bankruptcy discharge date, before you can apply for the loan. Foreclosures require 7 years from the foreclosure date. Some loans have more lenient guidelines and your loan officer should be able to outline this for you.

Amounts Owed-30%
The second-most important component of your credit score is how much you owe. Credit reporting agencies looks at the following factors:

- How much of your credit card limit is being used? This is called your credit utilization rate. Ideally, you should try to pay off your credit card/s on a monthly basis to avoid paying interest and keep your utilization rate low. But, if you need to carry a balance, try to keep your total debt below 30% of the credit limits. Anything above 30% is going to have a significant negative impact on your scores and, if you max-out your credit cards, you'll see an even more significant impact to your scores.
- How much do you owe on specific types of accounts, such as a mortgage, auto loans, credit cards and installment amounts? Credit scoring algorithms prefer you have a mix of different types of credit and that you manage them all responsibility.

Pro Tip There is a common misconception that it is a good thing to never use credit and avoid opening credit cards. The reason this can hurt you financially is that your credit scores are based purely on past credit in some shape or form; amount of credit, length of time having credit, ability to repay credit etc. If the credit bureaus have no information to review, they will not provide you with a score (literally your credit report will show a score of "N/A"). From a lender's perspective, they are unable to determine your credit worthiness and may in fact deny you solely on the fact you have never used credit. If you find yourself in a position where you do not have any credit whatsoever, you should speak with a loan officer about how you can rectify this situation. Usually it involves opening a small credit card, using it and paying it off each month. It could take some time for your credit profile to grow but the sooner you can start, the better.

Length of Credit History-15%
Your credit score also considers how long you have been using credit and how long your accounts have been open. A long history of having open credit, shows a prospective lender that over a long period of time, you can use credit and pay it back. Many first-time homebuyers do not have extensive credit histories because they only started acquiring and using debt when they became an adult.

Pro Tip if you are a younger buyer, ask your parents to be added on one of their credit cards as an authorized user. This will help to establish credit early and, assuming your parents have managed their debt well, your credit will reap the benefits. For parents reading this, you should consider doing this for your children to give them a head start as well. Of course, this comes with the added responsibility of making sure they are not using the card frivolously but the sooner they learn to manage debt, the better off they will be.

New Credit-10%
Opening new credit can have an impact on your credit scores. If you open 1 new account, it's not likely to have a significant impact on your scores because we all open new debt from time to time. But, if you open multiple accounts in a short period of time, the credit bureaus see this as a potential red flag. Someone that is opening 3 credit cards over the course of a week is likely in desperate need of liquidity and/or doesn't have the funds in checking/savings to cover this. Opening new debt, is common and can be beneficial to your credit but opening multiple accounts in rapid succession can drop your scores quickly.

Types of Credit in Use-10%
The final thing the credit scoring formulas consider is whether you have a mix of different types of credit, such as credit cards, store accounts, installment loans, and mortgages. It also looks at how many total accounts you have. Ideally, you should have a mix of credit accounts such as a car, a student loan and a couple credit cards. This shows you understand debt and can actively manage it.

How Home Appraisals Can Affect Your Home Loan

Most home loans require an appraisal to be completed during the underwriting process. The purpose of the appraisal is to determine the market value of the property and to confirm there are not qualitative issues that could impact that value. Different loan types have different criteria for what is an acceptable condition of the home but, the general rule of thumb is the property should be safe, sound and sanitary. Sometimes, the appraiser can make the determination that the value of the home is less than what has been agreed upon by buyer and seller as a sales price. If the home appraises for less than the sales price, one of the following may need to occur:

The homeowner reduces the selling price
Your real estate agent can reach out to the listing agent who can have a discussion with the seller about reducing the sales price to either match or split the difference between the sales price and appraised value. Of course,

most sellers will be reluctant to do this since it will result is less money in their pocket but if they review the appraisal (assuming you grant them access to the report) and they feel the comparable sales used to determine the subject property value are legitimate, they may be willing to negotiate the price down.

Ever situation is different and there is a very real chance they may not budge on the sale price which will require you to make a choice to proceed or back out of the contract. Therefore, it was mentioned earlier that a good agent will always include language in the contract that the buyer reserves the right to cancel the transaction if the home does not appraise at or above the sales price.

Assuming the seller has decided not to budge on the price and you still want to pursue the purchase of the home, you'll need to decide between one of these three options.

A higher down payment
Your lender structured your financing based on a loan amount as a percentage of the sales price. For example, let's assume you are buying the home for $200,000 and putting 5% ($10,000) down with a mortgage of $190,000. If the home appraises at $190,000, your lender will require 5% down of the lower of the sales price or appraised value, which is the $190,000 value. In other words, they will lend you $180,500 (95% of $190,000). If you have the financial capacity to put $19,500 down, you'll be able to secure the financing as originally structured. In doing so you'll need to consider the fact you are paying $200,000 for an asset valued at $190,000 which may or may not be in your best interest depending on your specific situation.

Dispute the appraisal
If you don't want to bring additional funds for the down payment and you feel as though there is inaccurate information used to appraise the home, your lender may be able to ask the appraiser to reconsider his value, commonly referred to as a rebuttal. This will require your agent to provide a list of comparable sales that they feel are more comparable than those used in the appraisal report or provide other supporting documentation/information to outline why the appraisal is not accurate.

In most cases, the appraiser holds firm with his initial report and does not update his value. The unfortunate nature of an appraisal is that it is an opinion of value and not something that can be precisely computed. For this reason, it is very difficult to dispute an appraisal and get the results you are hoping for.

Find another loan program or lender

If you the seller does not want to lower the sales price, you don't have (or want) to bring the larger down payment then the only other option would be to explore another loan program with a lower down payment requirement OR change lenders.

Since home appraisals are required by most lenders, you should find out during the loan application process the policies that the lender has when dealing with appraisers and appraisal issues. If the seller will not accept a lower sales price, the appraiser won't update his appraised value and your lender doesn't offer a lower down payment loan program then the last option would be to consider a different lender.

There is considerable risk in changing lenders because this may extend the closing date (which would need to be approved by the seller) and it may result in you paying for another appraisal that could come back with a similarly low valuation. Changing lender is a potential option but one that you need to give considerable though to before pursuing because of the added time and expense that may be lost.

Additional Fees for Home Loans

There are many parties involved in a home buying transaction. Some are those you meet such as your loan officer, real estate agent, closing attorney etc. while others are third parties such as the credit bureaus, title insurance companies, mortgage insurance companies etc. All these parties play a role and are compensated, usually, by you the buyer. Some of the fees include:

- Credit report fee
- Loan discount/origination fee
- Recording fee
- Appraisal fee
- Flood certificate
- Mortgage insurance application fee
- Assumption fee
- Hazard/Home insurance
- Title search
- Title insurance

These fees will be outlined on the initial disclosures you receive once you apply for your loan and will be updated throughout the process as amounts are updated and eventually finalized. At closing, you'll receive a Closing Disclosure (CD) which will have the final amounts in a detailed list. Please note, some of these fees are difficult to estimate at the start of the transaction while other are known immediately. Because of the variability of some fees, there are set tolerances that lenders must stay within from initial disclosure to closing. Gone are the days when you would arrive at closing to find out there is an extra lender fee of 1% (a point) being charged. These fees need to be presented to you before closing so you can make an informed decision about proceed with the financing.

Loan Estimate

Lenders use a form called the Loan Estimate (LE) to outline all the financial implications of the financing. This includes a breakdown of the monthly payment, the interest rate, the fees associated with the transaction and other important financial implications of the loan. The LE will be sent you with within 3 days of submitting a formal application. Most lenders send these electronically, but some still mail these forms through USPS or FedEx.

When looking for a lender, you should compare Loan Estimates to see which lender has the best financial package for your situation. It is important to pursue a loan with favorable financial terms, but you also want to make sure your lender can deliver on the terms being offered and on the dates you've agreed to in the purchase contract. In other words, many lenders may have rates/fees drastically lower than the other lenders you have spoken with. It's possible you may have simply found a great deal but it's also possible this lender has limited staff and has a very poor operation that could impact your transaction. In most cases, mortgages included, you get what you pay for!

Escrow and Other Loans Terms

As you are going through the home loan process, you will run across a few terms that may be foreign to you. You should ask your lender to explain these terms so that you understand the type of loan you are applying for, the lender policies, and other information that will be important throughout the life of the loan. Here are some common terms you may encounter:

Escrow

While this term can mean different things in different situations, you will see it often during the loan process. When you make an offer on a home you will usually be required to provide an initial deposit, commonly referred to as the Earnest Money Deposit (EMD). The EMD will be held in escrow until all the paperwork has been signed. The escrowed deposit money is held by a third party, such as the listing agent's brokerage or the seller's attorney. The individual or entity holding the funds is referred to as the escrow agent whereas the act of holding those funds and/or holding the property off the market, because its under contract, is referred to as being "in escrow."

Escrow is also a term that can mean funds being held by your lender for taxes and insurance. For most first-time buyers, you will be required to establish an escrow account with your lender that will be used to pay your homeowners insurance and real estate taxes as they come due. Usually, you will need to fund this escrow account with 2 months of taxes and 2 months of insurance premiums at closing. Thereafter, each month you will contribute 1/12 of the annual premiums so your lender will have the fund available to pay the taxes (quarterly) and the homeowner's insurance (annually). The funds held in this account are yours and you'll receive an escrow analysis form each year which outlines the money you paid into the account and the money that was paid out along with the remaining balance. Eventually when you refinance, sell or pay the loan off whatever remaining funds in the account will be reimbursed to you.

Mortgage

Mortgage is a term that is commonly used incorrectly. Many people think of a mortgage as a debt owed to a lender which is not entirely accurate. The Note is the obligation to repay a loan to a lender. A Mortgage is a security instrument that is recorded in town/city hall which outlines the rights and remedies of the lender in the event of default. The Mortgage and the Note are the two most important documents signed at closing as they outline the requirements to repay and the remedies in the event you fail to repay the loan.

Foreclosure

Foreclosure is the result of a borrower defaulting on the terms of the Note, generally for non-payment. Foreclosure rights are outlined in the Mortgage document and can result in the lender repossessing the home from the borrower. Foreclosures can stem from reasons besides non-payment such as using the property improperly or for illegal means. For example, if the borrower keeps 5 gallons of gas in their shed for their lawn mower, that's not an issue. If the borrower keeps 500 gallons of gas, which can be deemed hazardous, then the lender has the right to request the gas be removed with the threat of eventual foreclosure if the borrower is uncooperative.

Points
A point or a discount point is a fee charged by your lender for obtaining a certain interest rate on your behalf. Usually, 1 point is equal to 1% of the loan amount ($100,000 loan with 1 point would be a fee of $1,000) and usually results in an interest rate reduction of .125% - .375%. Everyone situation is different, but you should ask your lender to quote you rates with and without points to determine what option is best for you.

Debt to Income Ratio
A debt to income ratio (DTI) is the percentage of monthly expenditures divided by your monthly gross income. The debts included in your DTI are your projected mortgage payment (including property tax, insurance and PMI), auto loans, minimum credit card payments, personal/student loans and any other debts you have. It does not include non-essentials such as cable, cell phone, car insurance etc. If you add these debts up then divide by your gross income, you will compute your DTI. The general rule of thumb is to have your 'front-end' (housing-only) ratio below 31% and your 'back-end' (all debts) below 43%. There are many loan programs that offer looser guidelines than 31/43 but those are considered by most as affordable DTI ratios.

Private Mortgage Insurance
Private Mortgage Insurance (PMI) is an insurance a buyer pays when putting less than 20% down. This insurance protects the lender in the event the borrower defaults on the loan. PMI is a great tool for borrower with less than 20% down because it allows them to obtain the home without the substantial down payment. Conventional loans only require this premium to be paid until the borrower's loan-to-value reaches 80%, then PMI drops off. FHA has a similar Mortgage Insurance Premium (MIP) but the borrower pays this for the full life of the loan. There are ways to avoid paying PMI with less than 20% down and you should consult your loan officer to review those options to see if you qualify.

7
Making an Offer

If you've established your budget, met with your loan officer to get preapproved and met with your real estate agent to discuss what you are looking for, your next step may be to make an offer. Making an offer to buy a home can seem scary and overwhelming all at once but if you've done your homework that means you've put yourself in position to make an informed decision. Knowing this should put your mind at ease that this whole process isn't quite as scary as you may have thought before picking up this book. But there is still work to be done.

What to do Before Making an Offer

When you feel as though you have done your homework well enough to put you in a position that you are comfortable putting an offer on a home, there are some steps you should begin to take:

Attend open houses
Attend multiple open houses in the area where you want to live. This will give you the opportunity to see what is out there, the going price of homes in the area, and give you a basis of comparison when looking at other homes.

Research the property
If you find a home you might want to buy, you should find out everything you can about the property before making an offer. Visit the county clerk's office or land records office to see how much the current homeowners paid for the property, when they bought it and how many owners are there on record. Has the home sold every couple of years? If so, why? Has the current owner held onto the property for 20 years? If so, that is likely a good sign but that also might mean there hasn't been upgrades in recent years. Ask questions of the listing agent, Google search the current owners etc. Knowledge is power and the more power you have, the better your position to negotiate.

Find out more about taxes and utilities in the area
As a homeowner, you will be required to pay various taxes, such as, property tax, local tax, school tax, community/association dues, and other

taxes. Ask about the utilities available in the area as well. Some areas have well water while others have public water, some locations may have public sewers while others have septic or cesspool systems. Generally, the ideal utility set-up is public water, public gas and sewer. These are stress-free maintenance-wise and usually are the cheapest options as well. Before you commit to living in a certain area, make sure you understand the annual expenditures.

How to Write a Purchase Offer

This is an important step when making an offer to buy your first home. The purchase offer should outline everything you expect from seller and what they can expect from you. You should include the following in your offer:

- Offer price
- Amount of the initial deposit (EMD)
- Total down payment and amount financed along with the loan type you are apply for
- Contingencies (such as appliances that will stay, repairs that will need to be made, removal of items in the yard, etc.)
- Projected closing date
- Specify who will pay which fees and if there are any credits such as a seller closing cost credit
- Any inspections requested

You should try to be as specific as possible when writing up a purchasing offer. Each state has its own laws concerning contingency, amount of time a buyer must respond to the offer, and fees that are to be paid. Consult with your real estate attorney to get a better understand of these requirements.

Your real estate agent should be the one preparing the offer to purchase, with consultation from a local attorney if necessary, and presenting it on your behalf to the listing agent. Involving the title attorney at this stage is prudent because they may have some advice or additional contingencies they recommend you add depending on what you may be asking for regarding repairs, time frames etc. Once the offer is sent to the seller and both parties agree, it may be too late to make changes (without the seller's consent) so you want to be as thorough as possible from the start.

Low or High Offers

Hopefully, by researching the neighborhood and the property, you will be able to make a reasonable offer that is acceptable to the seller or at least an offer that warrants some negotiations. Depending on the state of the market (seller or buyer), your real estate agent should be able to advise you on whether a low-ball offer may be reasonable or not. It happens too often that buyers feel they can low ball sellers on any property to start the negotiations. It is true that a low-ball offer can sometimes be a starting point to a negotiation, it's also true that some sellers may simply disregard your offer if they deem it unreasonable. Conversely, some buyers may be so anxious to buy a home that they make an offer that is higher than what they are comfortable with because they are concerned they may lose the property. Understanding when to make a low or high offer is a tough skill to master but hopefully your real estate agent will have the experience to assist you in determined what the best offer tactic is.

How to Handle a Counteroffer and Offer Rejection

Sometimes, if you give a seller an offer that is lower than their asking price, they may counteroffer. Depending on the difference between your offer and their counteroffer, you may be able to continue the negotiations by offering another counteroffer to the seller but ever situation is going to be slightly different.

Counteroffer

Depending on where you live, the laws pertaining to counteroffers will vary. Typically, the number of counteroffers is limitless but if the parties are far apart, there will come a point of exhaustion where the parties will simply walk away. While counteroffers are usually focused on purchase price, these offers may also contain the following:

- Inclusion of appliances
- Repairs
- Time frame for closing
- Initial deposit amount

Buyers and sellers may only have hours to accept, reject, or present another counteroffer after receiving one. This can be a very stressful process, especially if you are dealing with a seller that has other offers on the table. While most homeowners will reject an offer if it is too low some will try to get the most they can from the sale and try to leverage multiple buyers to increase their offers by alerting them about the multiple offers.

Many times, this requires the listing agent to request a "highest and best" offer from all competing buyers by a specific time. When this occurs, the listing agent will be compiling all the offers then present them to the seller with their recommendation. You should not, it's not always just the highest purchase price that wins. Some sellers may be more willing to accept a lower offer with a conventional mortgage versus a slightly higher offer with an FHA mortgage. This is usually because FHA has a perception of being a difficult loan to get approval for (in reality, that is not always true).

Dealing with Rejection

The hardest part about an offer rejection is that the homeowner does not have to answer your offer. If you do not hear from the seller in a couple days, it is safe to assume they are not interested in your offer. While this can be frustrating, you need to move on. Again, try to keep the emotions on the side-lines during this part of the process. There will always be another home that meets your needs so stay positive and continue your home search.

If the seller gives you a response in the form of a rejection, they may site the reason why in the paperwork. If your offer was too low, they had another offer, decided not to sell, or want to wait for a higher offer, at least you can move on without wondering why your offer was rejected. Use this as a learning experience for the next time you make an offer.

Considering Items in the Home

When you are writing your purchase offer, you should consider the items that you would like to keep and items you would like to have removed from the home. These items can include:
- Certain appliances (such as washer and dryer)
- Lighting fixtures
- Storage fixtures
- Single air conditioning units that fit into windows
- Hardware from windows and doors
- Above ground pools and supplies

You should put these items in writing, so your request is clear. Some sellers may try taking certain items with them because they didn't know you wanted them or because they were not supposed to be sold with the home to begin with. Be sure to obtain a list of items the homeowner is selling with the home so that you can compare it to your list.

This can also work in reverse. If there are items that you would like removed from the property before you move in, you should specify these in the offer. These items can include:

- Old patio furniture
- Mechanical equipment
- Old appliances
- Light fixtures

By putting all these items in writing, you will be helping to move the buying process along. While the homeowners may not agree with everything that you may want to keep, it will be up to them if they want to continue the process. Having everything in writing will leave both parties with no surprises at closing.

Understanding the Seller

One key to making a solid offer is understanding the seller. Your real estate agent will be able to tell you a little bit about the seller that may help when trying to come up with a fair offer.

When deciding on an offer for the home, you should find out the following about the seller:

- How eager are they to sell their home?
- How long have they lived in the home?
- How long has the property been on the market? If it's been a while, why?
- How many offers have they received?
- How many have they turned down?
- Have they lowered their asking price?
- Are they relocating to another area?
- Do they need to sell their home quickly?

Understanding how to write up a contract, negotiate and come to terms with a seller is a very difficult task to do on your own. Therefore, having realtor working on your behalf is crucial to any real estate transaction. Many times, they are also able to help coach you through the frustrations of working with a difficult seller and/or deal with the heartbreak of losing out on a home you felt confident you were going to get.

8
Closing Day

Closing day is the culmination of a lot of hard work. From negotiating with the seller on price and inspection items to getting your mortgage loan fully underwritten and clear to close, there have been a lot of hurdles you jumped that all led up to this day.

Understanding the final steps before the day arrives will help to alleviate much of the anxiety that many buyers have on closing day.

Closing Disclosure and Final Cash to Close

The days leading up to the closing will usually focus on getting your financing finalized and receiving the 'clear to close' from your lender. The clear to close is the lender's classification for a file that has received full underwriting approval and is now ready to close.

Now that you know your loan is fully approved, you should expect to receive the Final Closing Disclosure (Final CD). The Final CD will reflect the terms, fees, prepaid items and exact cash to close you'll need to bring to closing. This amount should be fairly close to the original estimate provided at the time of application on your Loan Estimate (LE) and it should also be similar to what you saw on the Initial CD which is required to be sent to you at least 3 days prior to closing.

Your Final CD is an important document because it contains almost every important financial consideration related to this transaction. If there is any form you should review with a fine-tooth comb, it is the Final CD. Understanding this form in its entirety along with asking any questions you are uncertain of, will help to make this closing day go much smoother.

Once you've reviewed and feel comfortable with the amounts on the Final CD, you need to obtain a cashier's check or have a wire made payable to the closing attorney. PLEASE NOTE, whenever you are wiring monies, you will want to confirm the wiring instructions with the recipient, the closing attorney.

Final Walk Through

Now that you have the financing in order, your cashier's check for the cash to close in hand you are now ready for your final walkthrough. The final walkthrough is to ensure the property is still in the same condition as when you last saw it. You will also want to ensure that anything you have specifically requested, in the P&S, has been left or has been removed from the property. This is the reason why it is important to be very specific in the P&S so that there is no ambiguity during the walkthrough; if you specifically agreed to the washer and dryer remaining in the home, they should still be there. If you specifically requested that the shed be emptied and cleaned yet it is still full of junk, you will want to bring this up to the listing agent to figure out what can be done.

Here are some things you should make sure to check during your walkthrough:

- **Faucets and showers** – Make sure the water is running and you are getting hot and cold water.
- **Toilets** – Are they all flushing and is the tank refilling each time.
- **Air Conditioners** – Make sure these units are running and blowing cold air. Please note, A/C condensers need to be tested at 65 degrees or warmer so it is possible you may not be able to check this depending on the time of year.
- **Appliances** – Make sure they are all functioning as they were during your inspection.
- **Removal of Belongings** – The general rule of thumb is the property should be empty and in broom-swept condition. Ideally this will always be the case but many times you may need to accept the property in slightly less clean condition.
- **Lights** – Turn on every light switch to confirm they work.
- **Doors** – Open, close and lock each door to make sure there are no issues. This also applies to the garage doors.
- **Windows** – Test the windows to make sure they open, close and lock properly.

If there are issues with the property, you will want to bring these to the listing agent's attention as soon as possible. These can be worked out either through a credit from the seller, a holdback of the sellers proceeds until the work is completed (commonly referred to as an escrow holdback) or it may require the closing to be delayed or, worst case, cancelled. In most cases, these issues can be resolved with some negotiations so its important to be diligent during your walkthrough but it's also important to be reasonable. Every home that has been lived in should be expected to have some wear and tear. You'll need to make the decision as to whether the wear and tear is too significant for you to proceed with the purchase.

The Closing Table

Your financing is in order and the walkthrough was a success, next step is arriving at the closing table. Usually all parties are present at closing, including buyer, seller, both agents, the closing attorney, a seller's attorney and your lender. All these parties have played a role in getting you here and will likely be here for this last step as well.

Most of the time spent at closing, usually an hour or so, will be spent reviewing and signing the closing documents. There are some forms that both you and the seller will sign, other forms for the seller-only and some only for you, the buyer, to sign. The seller is usually only there for 15-20 minutes because the forms for the seller to sign are much less than yours, since most of your forms are related to the mortgage and the seller is not privy to those.

Once the seller has completed signing their portion, they will likely be ready to leave. This is an important time for you to ask any questions you may have such as:
- Do you have instruction manuals or paperwork for the appliances?
- Do you use a company for gas/oil/propane delivery?
- Do you have a company that services the sprinklers, pool, lawn care etc.?
- When is trash day?
- How are the neighbors?
- Does the garage or any of the doors have a code to get in? if so, what is it?

Every property is unique and has its own set of questions that comes along with it. Be prepared with your questions so that you respect the sellers time. Also, if the transaction went smoothly, you may want to ask if you can exchange contact information so you can reach out if there are any questions that come up later. If they are reluctant you can say you want to know so that you can reach out if any mail of theirs arrives at your home. This way they will see some value is sharing their info instead of just allowing you to reach out with questions.

Get Your Keys

The last step to the closing is receiving the keys from the seller. This is the final step in your home buying process. Getting the keys is a great feeling and one you'll likely never forget. Don't forget that you will want to have the doors re-keyed because you don't know who those keys were given out to by the seller during their time of ownership. Painters, contractors, family members etc. may all have copies of those keys and you will want to ensure your new home is only accessible to those you grant access to.

9
The 10 Essential Questions to Ask Your Real Estate Professional

1. How long have you been in the industry?

It's important to understand how long your loan officer has been assisting clients with their financing needs. The mortgage market has grown in complexity in recent years and being new to loan origination may make navigating guidelines, product matrices and setting proper expectations quite difficult. This is not to say that newer loan officers can't do a great job and fit you into the right product. That would be disingenuous just like saying every seasoned loan officer will be great to work with and knows everything there is to know about mortgages. Understanding the experience level of your loan officer will help to ensure expectations are set up-front which is crucial to a pleasant home buying experience.

2. What makes you competitive and why should I choose you as my loan officer/lender?

Let's face it, the mortgage loan as a product has been commoditized to an extent. There is no shortage of mortgage lenders willing to offer you a loan to help with your home purchase and the question which most lenders are rated by, "what interest rate can you offer," usually is answered with very similar responses. It's rare that you'll call Lender A and receive a quote that is more than +/- .125% different than Lender B's offering.

So why not just go with the first lender you call? Well that is where differentiation comes into play. Asking what sets them apart instead of the standard "what rate are you offering" question will open your eyes to aspects you may not have considered, such as, the length of time to close the loan or the amount of communication with all parties during the process. Anyone that has gone through the loan process knows that a quick and efficient process is incredibly valuable, yet many first-time buyers don't know to ask about it.

Knowing more about the company, its process and the qualitative aspects that make them competitive is just as important, if not more so, than the quantitative aspects. How can Lender A close 8 loans a month when

Lender B only closes 2? There could be a multiple reason to explain this difference and finding out exactly what they are will be crucial when picking a lender. Maybe Lender A is available, day/night/weekends while Lender B leaves the office at 5pm and can't be reached until the morning. Maybe Lender A has mastered his loan process and is able to close loans quickly and efficiently which leads to his realtors trusting him more with their referrals.

Understanding why you should work with a loan officer often starts with asking what makes them different and how their value proposition can benefit you. If rate is your only focus you may find the loan process to be difficult, time consuming and a regretful experience.

3. What does your process look like and how does that compare to the industry?

The aspect of mortgage lending that is questioned least but should warrant the most focus is the loan approval process – from application to closing. No two lenders are alike, and their mortgage processes are likely quite different as well.

Some lenders prefer to underwrite the file up-front or during the preapproval stage, while others wait until the file has passed through multiple stages before its reviewed by an underwriter. Depending who you ask you'll get a different response as to which approach is best but, regardless of opinions, you need to have a clear understanding of what your process will look like. This will help to set proper expectations and will keep your loan officer accountable to ensure all the contractual dates and obligations are met. Understanding the process from the start will be in everyone's best interest.

Pro Tip ask your loan officer if he would be comfortable outlining the process on a monthly calendar with you. This exercise will provide a roadmap for you and your loan officer to follow, ensuring everything stays on track. Of course, with so many moving pieces it is perfectly understandable for things to shift slightly but having an outline from the start should keeping things moving along in a timely manner.

4. Do you have any review/testimonials from past clients?

In the age of the internet we have more information at our fingertips than ever before, and savvy homebuyers should be taking advantage of this when considering a lender. Reviewing online real estate sites such as Zillow and Trulia along with social media and search engine pages like Facebook, Instagram and Google should give you some insight into the experiences of past clients and how they felt about working with this real estate professional.

The truth of the matter is if the real estate professional is doing right by other clients, those folks will likely be willing to write reviews for them and provide information you may find helpful in determining which real estate partner to work with.

Please note, as with any online review, you need to take them with a grain of salt. A strong real estate professional usually has multiple reviews so if they have 30 5-Star reviews but then you see a 1-Star review that makes the professional appear to be less than ideal to work with then you may want to rule that one out. There are so many things that can go wrong during a transaction and many times they are out of the control of those involved. For example, if an appraisal report comes back with a low value which ends up negatively impacting the deal, it can reflect poorly in a client's review of the Loan Officer because they are the face of the company that ordered the appraisal. Likely there is nothing that loan officer could do to prevent such an issue from occurring. If the loan officer went as far as submitting a rebuttal that was denied, their hands are then tied.

Reviews are an important tool to use when considering a real estate professional but it's important to be open-minded when considering them.

5. What is your availability?

In a sellers-market, one in which sellers hold the bargaining power, it is very important to work with a real estate agent and loan officer that are available outside of normal business hours. Of course, there is nothing wrong with a real estate professional who draws certain lines in the sand with the time they devote to work as we all need time to spend with our family and friends. But you need to understand that availability can be the difference between you getting the home or losing out to someone working with a more aggressive real estate partner.

Real estate is a business that never sleeps; there are always new properties coming to market, prices being updated and deals coming together. If your agent is unable to quickly contact a listing agent or your loan officer takes too long to update a preapproval letter, you may miss out.

Open houses are generally set for Saturday and Sunday mornings meaning offers are usually formulated those same afternoons and if you need to wait until Monday/Tuesday to present your offer you may have missed out. This isn't to say that knee-jerk reaction is always required but ask any good agent how quickly the last home that was priced well in a nice neighborhood went from "New Listing" to "Pending" and I bet it was in a flash!

Availability and strong communication skills are quite possibly the two most important traits any good real estate professional possesses. Offering the lowest commission or the cheapest interest rate doesn't mean much if you aren't able to get an accepted offer to purchase the property.

6. Do you work with first time buyers often, and if so, how do you feel you are best equipped to assist me on this journey to homeownership?

Let's face it, we all have our strengths and weaknesses. For some, patience is not their strong suit. As a first-time homebuyer, patience is a key trait to look for in your real estate professional. We all had the same questions when we bought our first home so you should never feel as though you are asking a foolish question.

Making a purchase, likely in the 6-figure range, should not be a decision taken lightly. Understanding every aspect of a purchase of this magnitude will pay dividends for years to come. Many real estate professionals may not be capable (or willing) to devote the time and energy required to fully equip a first-time buyer with the information necessary to properly prepare them for this purchase.

You can generally identify a real estate professional who works well with first time buyers as those that first listen, then follow up with questions and finally provide advice. Finding a real estate professional that is willing to devote this level of focus to your scenario is going to ensure you are properly prepared to move forward with a home purchase.

7. Do you have contacts that could assist me with aspects beyond the financing and real estate purchase such as insurance agents, contractors etc.?

Real estate agents and loan officers with good reputations will likely have referral partners with similar reputations. There are so many fields that are interrelated in the real estate market it could make your head spin so having real estate partners that have reputable contacts in these various fields will make your transaction much more enjoyable and will also help during your time as the homeowner. To name a few:

- **Homeowners Insurance Agent** – You'll be required (and want) to buy a homeowner's insurance policy to protect your new home from damage, theft, floods etc.
- **Financial Advisors** – Maybe the most overlooked piece of buying a piece of real estate is that you now have a huge liability that could be left on your family's balance sheet in the event something happened to you. Having a financial plan in place to prevent this is very important.
- **Real Estate Attorney** – Having an attorney that understands real estate law and practices on a regular basis is important to protect your interest in the transaction and during your time as the homeowner. Most first-time buyers do not understand title insurance and having a reputable attorney explain and provide this product will be crucial to your home buying experience.
- **Carpenters, Electricians, Plumbers Etc.** – Everyone knows someone in these various fields but not everyone has someone that is reliable and answers the phone. As a tenant, you simply call the landlord and it's on them to take care of it but, as a homeowner, you need to have these contacts and need to know you can trust them to be responsive.

8. Why did you get into the mortgage/real estate industry?

If the answer to this question is money, head for the door. There is no doubt that you can have great success in real estate which will lead to a very lucrative career but those that are in it solely for the money are considered transactional not relational. In other words, they see your home purchase as a transaction or dollar-signs opposed to seeing your purchase as an opportunity to help you obtain your dream home...there is a BIG difference there.

You want your real estate partner to be interested in your goals and be involved from the day you meet until the day they retire. Real estate is an always evolving field and its quite likely that you will buy multiple properties during your life. You may buy this home with your agent and loan officer, then after a few years your family has grown which requires up-sizing. Then your kids are off to college, so you need a cash-out refinance to pay for their tuition. Next is retirement planning which allows for that second home by the ocean and a home equity line for traveling on that condo you bought as an investment property.

Having someone who sticks with you throughout these various life events, keep you up to date with market trends and is generally interested in your real estate needs would be the description of someone who is relational instead of transactional. Look for someone that is looking out for you instead of themselves and you'll find yourself making informed real estate decisions.

9. What is the value you bring over doing my own research online?

There has been a growing trend over the last few years where buyers/sellers are wondering what value a real estate agent and/or loan officer can bring to the table compared to online lenders and real estate sales platforms (think Quick Loans, Zillow, Trulia etc.). If you ask your real estate professional what they bring to the table compared to an online sales platform and they can't give you an answer, that is a problem!

The truth is many real estate professionals can't provide more value than an online portal because they are either ill equipped, lazy or don't have the time and/or desire to do so. The consummate real estate professional should always be able to outshine the online competitors. The online folks are unable to replicate the emotion that comes along with real estate transactions. Whether or not you want to accept it now, real estate is a very emotional transaction. There are families being uprooted and relocated thus changing jobs, schools and friends. These moves are often contingent upon successful closings on another home and often time require the precision of a finely tuned German sports car. If one thing goes wrong, there can be a domino effect that can dramatically impact multiple parties and result in significant financial complications.

Having a local real estate professional can help to steer the ship much easier than someone located across the country or, even worse, software that treats you as though you are a transaction instead of a person. Online research is important and should be done by anyone interested in buying/selling a home but there has yet to be any software written that can replace the boots on the ground of a relationship based real estate partner who has your local knowledge and your best interest in mind.

10. Do you have a specialty?

Understanding if your real estate professional has a specialty is important to ensure their skills match your needs and desires. Hiring a real estate agent who specializes in multi-family investment properties to help you buy a single-family primary residence in a rural part of the state may not be in your best interest. Of course, this is not to say an agent can't do both well but it's important to ask the question, so you know up-front what their strengths and weaknesses are.

As a loan officer, I can write mortgages in any state I want to get licensed in. I purposefully do not intend on obtaining my real estate license in most states because I do not consider myself an expert in the majority of states and want to keep my focus on the northeast and Florida (for snowbirds). Most real estate professional will consider themselves a specialist in a certain aspect of the market or geographic area and knowingly exactly what that is can help you make the most informed decision as to whether you work with them.

10
Conclusion

Buying your first home can be one of the most stressful and frustrating processes you ever go through if you do not align yourself with a lender and real estate agent that are looking out for your best interest. You will undoubtedly have questions and need guidance at almost every step of the process but if you have a team in place to be your guide, you will be glad you did.

I hope reading this book has provided you with some insights into what you should expect as a first time home buyer but I also hope it reinforced the value of the consummate profession real estate partner and why it is so important to work with them.

If there is ever an opportunity for me to further assist you, even if you decide not to work with me, I would be happy to provide sound advice and guidance at your convenience. As a mortgage professional my hope is to build relationship. Getting to know you, your family and your goals is why I love what I do.

Past Client Testimonials

Best experience ever

mmarte1011 from Johnston, RI

Nate is was the best, I will recommend him and Movement 100%. Nate was there for me every step of way for me. The process was smooth and the online application was easy to follow and complete. Movement was clear on what I needed in order to close, and Nate was super helpful making clear my options and which one fit my current needs and wants. I was able to reach out to him for any questions and he would reach out within a day.

LOAN STATUS Closed Sep 2019   INTEREST RATE Lower than expected

LOAN TYPE Refinance   FEES/CLOSING COSTS As expected

CLOSE ON TIME Yes

Exceptional service

Sapna J from East Providence, RI

Nate is exceptional at what he does and I am so happy to work with him. He is quick, professional, responsive and goes above and beyond to get the job done. He came to my place on a Sunday to explain all the details of my closing. Given the super narrow time frame of just a couple of weeks, I am very thankful to Nate that he took care of everything in time. Nate made the tedious process of home buying very easy and stress free for me. Because of my pleasant experience with Nate, I highly recommend him to anybody who is looking to shop for mortgage. You won't be disappointed. THANK YOU Nate! If I ever have to make this purchase again, I know without doubt where to go. I will send some referrals your way!

LOAN STATUS Closed Jun 2018   INTEREST RATE As expected

LOAN TYPE Purchase   FEES/CLOSING COSTS Lower than expected

CLOSE ON TIME Yes

★★★★★ 4 months ago

My fiancé and I bought our first home and luckily we had the opportunity to work with Nate. He is very knowledgeable, friendly and was always available to answer all our questions. He also made the home buying process look easy and went a step further to ensure our rate and closing costs were the best available.

Home Finance ROCK STAR

Dave McCormick from Tiverton, RI

After arriving in the area for a military assignment, my prior arrangements for a rental house fell through. We had no place to live, and needed to get into a residence fast. Nate was recommended by our realtor. I called him out of the blue, asking if he could help with a fast-track home purchase. Nate flew into action and began guiding us through the very complex home financing process. He communicated with me several times each day, relaying information and documents as necessary to avoid delays. He worked long hours, promptly answering my texts and emails at all times of day. He met with me in person in order to expedite some documents. Nate demonstrated his experience and expertise at every turn. He is a home finance rock star. In summary, we ended up closing in a very short time with a very favorable rate.

LOAN STATUS Closed Jun 2019	INTEREST RATE Lower than expected
LOAN TYPE Purchase	FEES/CLOSING COSTS As expected
CLOSE ON TIME Yes	

★★★★★ 4 months ago

It was great working with Nate, I needed to have a quick closing with no surprises and Nate made it happen. He worked hard to keep everything transparent and kept me informed every step of the way. This is the way buying a home should be. Keep up the good work. Thanks Nate.

Trustworthy, Honest & Professional

Jessica Hicks from North Providence, RI

Nate was there every step of the way during the process of buying our first home. He explained everything and made the process of getting our loan a lot less painful. Nate was always one step ahead and made sure we knew what we would need to make the process go smoothly and efficiently. He is very knowledgeable and always had the answer to our questions. Nate always was available to answer calls, emails, or texts no matter what time of day. This made our process a lot less stressful and we couldn't have been happier with everything he did for us. Having a lender we felt comfortable with helped ease our anxiety of buying our first home, we would highly recommend Nate for your lending needs. Look no further, Nate will make your transaction a quick and painless one.

LOAN STATUS Closed Mar 2019	INTEREST RATE Lower than expected
LOAN TYPE Purchase	FEES/CLOSING COSTS As expected
CLOSE ON TIME Yes	

Made in the USA
Columbia, SC
26 September 2024